SKY WOLF'S CALL

THE GIFT OF INDIGENOUS KNOWLEDGE

ELDON YELLOWHORN & KATHY LOWINGER

annick
press
toronto · berkeley

To Peter Kalman, and in memory of Susan Juhasz and Vecsei Mari —KL

To Eva, and all my relations —EY

Pages 114 to 115 constitute an extension of this copyright page.

Cover art credits: (man) Danita Delimont / Alamy Stock Photo; (wolf) Taylor/Unsplash;
    (moon cycle) Adam Dutton/Unsplash
Text design and layout by Tania Craan
Photo research by Mary Rose MacLachlan, Mac/Cap Permissions
Edited by Chandra Wohleber
Copy edited by Lisa Frenette
Proofread by Doeun Rivendell
Index by Wendy Thomas

With special thanks to Api'soomaahka (William Singer III) for his review of the text.

Annick Press Ltd.

We acknowledge the support of the Canada Council for the Arts and the Ontario Arts Council, and the participation of the Government of Canada/la participation du gouvernement du Canada for our publishing activities.

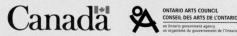

Library and Archives Canada Cataloguing in Publication

Title: Sky Wolf's call : the gift of Indigenous knowledge / Eldon Yellowhorn, Kathy Lowinger.
Names: Yellowhorn, Eldon, 1956- author. | Lowinger, Kathy, author.
Identifiers: Canadiana (print) 20210328827 | Canadiana (ebook) 20210328851 | ISBN 9781773216300
    (hardcover) | ISBN 9781773216294 (softcover) | ISBN 9781773216324 (PDF) | ISBN 9781773216317
    (HTML)
Subjects: LCSH: Ethnoscience—Canada—Juvenile literature. | LCSH: Ethnoscience—United States—
    Juvenile literature. | LCSH: Indigenous peoples—Canada—Juvenile literature. | LCSH: Indigenous
    peoples—United States—Juvenile literature.
Classification: LCC GN476 .Y35 2022 | DDC j500.89/97—dc23

Published in the U.S.A. by Annick Press (U.S.) Ltd.
Distributed in Canada by University of Toronto Press.
Distributed in the U.S.A. by Publishers Group West.

Printed in China

annickpress.com
Also available as an e-book. Please visit annickpress.com/ebooks for more details.

CONTENTS

AUTHOR'S NOTE

Indigenous people are the subjects of this book. Although everyone has a name for their own culture, we use this phrase to be inclusive. In the past, writers used names such as Indian, Native, First Nations, and Aboriginal. Canadian law still uses the term "Indian" in the Indian Act, so we have left this name intact. "Canada" and "the United States" and the current names of towns and rivers overshadow the borders, place names, and geography that Indigenous people once knew. Although they are recent we use modern maps here to help you locate the places we describe.

You'll see we use the terms "nation", "band", and "tribe." Here's what they mean. Nation refers to a group of people who are identified with a particular territory. A band is a small, self-governing group that bases its membership on family connections. In Canada a band has a legal meaning as a political unit occupying an "Indian reserve," though we now call them First Nations. Tribe describes a collection of bands connected by kinship, politics, and language. The United States has a legal definition for a political unit associated with an "Indian reservation."

Blackfoot and Blackfeet are political names. We call ourselves *Niitsitapi* and our language is *Niitsi'poysin*, but Canadians know us and our language by the name "Blackfoot." "Blackfeet" is the name used in Montana. Today Blackfoot, which comes from the word *siksika* (it means "black foot"), is a language in danger of falling silent, but it is our mother tongue whether we are called Blackfoot or Blackfeet.

Sky Wolf's Call

The Gift of Indigenous Knowledge

Heiltsuk First Nation students from the Bella Bella Community School SEAS program explore the estuary of a nearby salmon stream.

THE SKY WOLF'S CALL:
The Gift of Indigenous Knowledge

The United States recognizes 573 tribes, and Canada shares the land with about 600 First Nations. We practice diverse cultures, and we speak many languages.

Indigenous knowledge comes from years of practices, experiences, and ideas gathered by people who have a long history with the natural world. Indigenous knowledge comes from many distinct communities, but it braids together these ideas:

Everything is connected.
The world is a gift.
The sacred is a vital part of knowing.
We are always learning.

How do these ideas, or principles, turn into action?

Tree of Life, by Donald Chrétien (Anishinaabe), acrylic on canvas

Everything Is Connected

Humankind has not woven the web of life.
We are but one thread within it.
Whatever we do to the web, we do to ourselves.
All things are bound together.
All things connect.
> —Chief Seattle, Suquamish and Duwamish
> Chief, Washington State, 1786–1866

Everything is connected: Plants grow from the soil and support all creatures whether they are two-legged or four-legged, or have wings or crawl on the ground. They are all braided together into the web of life.

Let's follow one of countless threads of connection—the one that joins pecans and squirrels. Squirrels love pecans, even though they have hard shells. Pecans are rich in protein, fat, and vitamins and are perfect winter food for hungry squirrels. In some years, pecan trees produce lots of nuts, and in other years, very few. If a squirrel spends a lot of time on a tree branch gnawing through the pecan shell, it is easy prey for a hawk. Storing pecans softens the shells, and the squirrel can safely feed on them in its nest.

The pecans help squirrels, and by storing the nuts, squirrels help pecan trees. If every pecan were to begin a new tree, they would crowd each other and none would survive. Those pecans left on the forest floor after squirrels have gathered what they need will have plenty of room to start healthy new trees that will produce more pecans. By following this one thread, we can see that the well-being of the trees, the forest, and the squirrels are intertwined.

This World Is a Great Gift

The Potawatomi people, who live on the Great Plains, the upper Mississippi River, and the Western Great Lakes, call the land *emingoyak*, which means "that which has been given us" in their language. Indigenous knowledge teaches us that the world is a gift.

You know how to act when someone gives you a gift. You say, "Thank you." You take special care of it. And the time comes for you to give a gift in return. That is how we should act when we receive the earth's gifts: with thanks, with care, and by giving back. This is the belief that preserves the Menominee Forest.

Potawatomi Gathering is hosted each year by one of the nine bands of Potawatomi, providing an opportunity for members of all bands to come together and celebrate their Potawatomi heritage.

The lands of the Menominee Nation once covered 4 million hectares (10 million acres) in what is Wisconsin and Upper Michigan today. Now the people live on the 95,100-hectare (235,000-acre) Menominee Reservation in northeastern Wisconsin. At the heart of the reservation is a forest. In 1854, the Menominee bought a small sawmill to cut and process lumber.

The Menominee take good care of the forest. They allow some trees to reach full maturity before they are cut down for the sawmill. Other trees are never cut down so that thriving stands of old-growth white pine and sugar maple remain. Some white pine stands are more than two centuries old, and the hemlocks are even older. The Menominee make sure that the forest is diverse. At least thirty different kinds of trees, including white pine, hemlock, Canada yew, sugar maple, aspen, oak, and hickory, grow there. And they never chop down more trees than necessary, so future generations will always have a supply of timber.

By taking care of the trees, the Menominee are taking care of the animals and the water, too. Dozens of species of plants and animals, including bears, otters, and birds, thrive in their forest home.

The result: The forest gives the Menominee income from the sawmill, and with the Menominee taking care of the forest, there are more trees now than when the sawmill started operating. And the forest will continue to flourish so that the next seven generations will also benefit.

The Importance of the Sacred

When Blackfoot speakers say *naato*, it means "sacred" or "holy." We use words like "spiritual" or "sacred" to express our belief that there is a power greater than ourselves.

THE SEVENTH GENERATION PRINCIPLE

The Seventh Generation Principle means thinking about how our actions will affect future generations.

Loggers use sustainable harvesting techniques to preserve the forest. Menominee Tribal Enterprises employs careful precision to sustainably harvest the Menominee Forest.

© Frank Vaisvilas – USA Today Network

Cliff Palace, located in Mesa Verde National Park, Colorado, was built by ancient Pueblo people, and is the largest cliff dwelling in North America.

The sacred is braided into every kind of Indigenous knowledge, even our homes. For example, the doors to our tipis must always face east to greet the rising sun with our prayers. However, there is a practical reason for this, too, since our tipis protect us from the prevailing westerly winds.

In the Southwest, Pueblo engineers, architects, and craftspeople built four- and five-story dwellings—the first apartments in the world—where thousands of people lived. They also built circular, underground ceremonial rooms called kivas for their religious ceremonies. The buildings were so well constructed that a thousand years later, people in Taos Pueblo still live in them.

People climbed between the floors of their homes and in and out of kivas using rope and wood ladders. The ladders were made of pine and spruce brought from hundreds of miles away. In the desert country of the Southwest, wood was hard to come by. People had to travel great distances to cut it. Then they had to haul it home. Sometimes they might save themselves the work by trading for wood.

They did so because the ladders had spiritual meaning. Their oral tradition told them that humans first emerged from the underworld to this one by climbing a reed or notched piece of wood. When Pueblo people climbed the ladders from one floor to the next, they were connecting with the sacred way their ancient ancestors climbed out of the earth.

Blackfoot tipis in Alberta

We Are Always Learning

Indigenous knowledge is always growing and adapting. We have a long history of adopting new ideas and "repurposing" them. The Mi'kmaq call this practice *Etuapmumk*, or "two-eyed seeing."

Adapting Ideas

Chocolate is a delicious example of how ideas were adopted and adapted.

Cacao trees come from the Amazon and Orinoco river basins in South America. People gathered the cacao pods, ate the sweet pulp, and threw away the seeds or beans. Around five thousand years ago people in the Yucatán Peninsula imported the trees. They removed the *kakawa* (cacao) beans, dried them in the sun, and then they roasted them. Finally they ground the beans into a dark paste that they formed into patties. It tasted bitter, so they mixed it with honey or vanilla or chili peppers. The result? A drink they loved. They especially liked froth and would stand on something high while pouring it to make as much froth as possible.

The taste for chocolate quickly spread north along trade routes. By one thousand years ago, 4,800 kilometers (3,000 miles) north of the nearest chocolate plantation, people in the pueblos of Mesa Verde and Chaco Canyon were enjoying chocolate.

Repurposing Ideas

Indigenous knowledge is fluid—we know how to repurpose ideas when our needs change. In the far north, for centuries Inuit used a *qulliq*, which is a type of oil lamp made of soapstone and an arctic cotton and moss wick fueled by animal oil. A lit *qulliq* can heat a home, dry clothes, and cook food. Inuit no longer rely on the *qulliq* for those purposes, but they have not forgotten them. Now the *qulliq* is used as a teaching tool and as part of ceremonies where it is a sacred symbol of Inuit identity.

This 15th- or 16th-century Aztec statue of a man carrying a cacao pod is made of volcanic stone with traces of red pigment.

Inuit woman lights a *qulliq* to greet visitors to the High Arctic. The *qulliq* (Inuit lamp) symbolizes Inuit women's strength, care, and love. The *qulliq* represent the light and warmth provided at the hearth. The lamp is made for a woman as a gift from her husband. Then, as the owner, she becomes the flame keeper.

Mi'kmaw Elder Albert Marshall

Etuapmumk, Two-Eyed Seeing

Etuapmumk means "two-eyed seeing" in the Mi'kmaq language. One eye sees with the strengths of Indigenous ways of knowing, and the other eye sees a scientific worldview. *Etuapmumk* means learning to use both eyes together for the benefit of all.

Mi'kmaw Elder Albert Marshall describes the practice: "When we braid Indigenous science with Western science, we acknowledge that both ways of knowing are legitimate forms of knowledge . . . The more something is shared, the greater becomes its value."

Just one example: The Arctic will be the first place to experience the full impact of climate change. Inuit who live there have documented how sea ice conditions have changed. They observe how animals, birds, and fish have altered their migration patterns. They share this valuable knowledge with research scientists to show how the warmer conditions directly affect their lives.

ELDERS AND KNOWLEDGE KEEPERS

The term "Elder" doesn't necessarily mean that a person is old. It is given to an individual by their community because of the spiritual and cultural knowledge they hold.

Knowledge Keepers are people who have been taught by an Elder or a senior Knowledge Keeper within their community. This person holds and cares for traditional teachings, and shares their knowledge with others when the time is right.

Tatigat, an Inuk, cracks his whip to encourage his dog team over the ice near Igloolik. Nunavut.

SKY WOLF'S CALL

Indigenous knowledge is held in our stories, the teachings of our Elders and Knowledge Keepers, our practices, and our own experiences and observations. That's why you'll find examples of them all in this book.

Our stories are funny, serious, scary, and entertaining so that we will remember them.

On the prairies many of our stories are about a kindly cultural hero called Naapi, who is sometimes a troublemaker, a trickster, or foolish. He made a new world for us, but our early ancestors didn't always heed his vital lessons. How did they learn to live in the world? When Naapi was not around, a pack of wolves came down from the Sky Country. Their gift of knowledge taught us how to live together on the earth, so we have named our book after them. This is their story.

STORIES

Every nation has its own stories and the right to use them. They can only be reproduced with permission from that nation. The traditional stories you find here are from my Piikani heritage.

Dressed in traditional clothing, three Blackfoot girls play hand drums and sing handed-down songs in Browning, Montana.

Long ago the sky and the earth were the same place. Humans and Star People lived next to each other.

Then, some human children killed a Star Boy. Sun and the Star People decided that humans could not be trusted. They pulled the sky away from the earth. Then they sent a great storm to destroy the world with a flood.

Naapi was a Star Man who loved the humans he had befriended. Though he tried hard, he couldn't save them. He barely saved himself by climbing to a high mountaintop. Quickly, he built a raft from some logs he found. As he floated on his raft, some of his animal friends joined him.

Although he survived the flood, he did not want to join the Star People in their Sky Country. Sun, the Chief of the Star People, gave Naapi the power to create.

Naapi made a new world and he made people to live on it. He gave the people speech and language. He taught them how to gather food. He taught them how to build homes.

When Naapi was sure that his people could live on their own, he told them that he wanted to go and see the world he had created. His people assured him that they could take care of themselves.

But troubles began soon after Naapi left. The people did not cooperate for their hunting, so their hunting failed, and they had no food. Their children cried with hunger. Without the hides of animals, they could not make their clothes or build their tipis. Day by day their grief increased. They wished Naapi would come back to them.

Up in the Sky Country there lived a pack of wolves. The wolves had known Naapi from the time when the sky and earth were one place. The wolves saw that Naapi's people were in distress. They traveled down to Naapi's world to help.

The Sky Wolves lived among Naapi's people. They showed them how to cooperate when they hunted. They taught the people how to be good parents to their children. They taught the ways of living a good life. Once the Sky Wolves were sure the people could live on their own, they prepared to return to their home in the sky.

Before they traveled their Wolf Road back to the Sky Country, they had one last gift for the people. They left behind the gift of song. Singing together taught the people to enjoy the company of visitors. They learned to dance together—dancing encourages friendship.

To this day, Blackfoot people recall that gift when they bring out their drums to sing. We invite old and new friends to join us in our powwows, and we remember the Sky Wolves' lessons.

The Grand Entry of Dancers in full regalia at the Blackfoot Arts & Heritage Festival Pow Wow in Waterton Lakes National Park, Alberta

Indigenous knowledge in the Blackfoot tradition began with the Sky Wolves' lessons. Today our task is to transform those principles into actions. We start with water. Lakota of North and South Dakota have a saying, "Water is life."

At Writing-on-Stone Provincial Park in Alberta, Mars can be seen to the left of the galactic center area of the Milky Way.

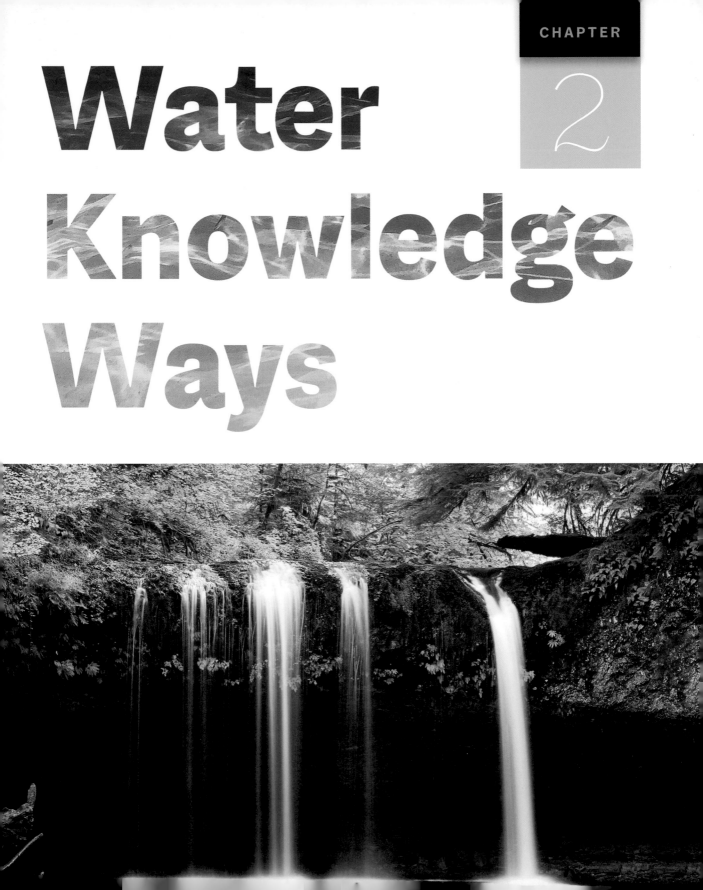

Water Knowledge Ways

Every living thing is connected by the need for water. In dry lands, seeds can lie dormant for years until a storm brings rain. When rain wakes them up, flowers bloom again. No animal can survive without water. Water makes up roughly 60 percent of the human body. Though people can live for weeks without food, most of us would die if we went for more than three days without a drink. Water is so powerful that rivers, oceans, and streams carve out canyons and mountains. It is one of the forces shaping the earth itself.

SACRED WATER

On the Great Plains, my ancestors believed that there were three separate sacred realms: the earth, the sky, and water. Water was scarce and it needed special attention. Water is sacred because it is home to divine beings that instructed people to protect the water world. Killing and eating creatures that live in water was not a Piikani custom. Even today we oppose dams that disturb the flow of rivers, or pipelines that might pollute them.

The story of Beaver describes the connection between water, humans, and beavers.

Beaver dam construction near Hinton, Alberta

The Beaver's Lesson

After the Star People had torn the sky from the earth and sent the storm that drowned the world, Sun invited Naapi to join the other Star People in Sky Country, but Naapi refused. So, Sun gave Naapi the power to remake the earth.

Naapi told his animal friends on the raft that he needed mud from the old world to make a new world. They agreed to dive down to retrieve the mud.

Muskrat dove first, but though he swam deep, he could find no mud. Loon tried next, and after him, Otter, but the water was too deep. At last, Beaver took his turn. He was gone for a long, long time—so long that he drowned. When his body floated to the surface, Naapi and the animals pulled it onto the raft. They found Beaver with a clump of mud clutched in his paw.

Naapi restored Beaver's life by sharing the spirit of breath. Then he took the mud, rolled it between his hands, and threw it back into the water. It did not sink. Instead, it grew larger and larger until they could step onto solid ground. That was the beginning of land. Grateful Naapi made Beaver the Chief of the Water People and gave him the power to control the flow of water.

The beaver, an animal that lives in the water and on the land, reminds us that the water and land are linked with each other. The story reminds us that animals and people are part of the same circle. If we take care of the water, we take care of ourselves and our animal relatives.

The story is also a practical lesson about how to conserve precious fresh water in a dry landscape. To this day, when beavers build their dams, they create homes for many other animals: muskrats, otters, and water birds. When they build dams on creeks and rivers, they create ponds of fresh water where plants grow and wildlife can thrive.

WATER KNOWLEDGE IN ACTION

Indigenous people used their water knowledge in many ways. The Hohokam in the dry Southwest found ways to irrigate their crops. In Nova Scotia, water knowledge gave Mi'kmaq the ability to travel great distances on waterways. In Florida, water shaped what the Calusa ate, the houses they lived in, and even the battles they fought.

The Hohokam Canals

Some of the most outstanding examples of ancient water knowledge come from the deserts of the Southwest. Around 300-750 CE the Hohokam started farming corn and other plants on the floodplains of the Gila and Salt rivers, but seasonal flooding kept wiping out their crops. The rest of the year was dry. They solved the problem by building 1,100 kilometers (700 miles) of irrigation canals to divert water from the rivers and bring it to their fields. The canals were so well made that mid-19th-century settlers in what is now called Phoenix, Arizona, repaired and used them to water their farms. The ancient canals are still part of the city's water management system.

Their canals were the work of skilled engineers and of people who did the hard labor of digging the canals using nothing but wooden digging sticks. Constructing them took immense effort: Even a small canal took 25,000 hours to construct. Many of the canals were 13 to 19 kilometers (8 to 12 miles) long.

There were at least seventeen Hohokam multi-village irrigation communities that built and repaired the canals so they could share the water fairly. When they diverted water from the rivers, they also captured fish that swam into their canals. They could supplement their diets of corn, beans, and squash with the fish they caught, which was an important source of protein for farmers.

Mi'kmaw Water Highways

The Mi'kmaq live on the Atlantic coast of North America. Those who lived in Nova Scotia had a way of life closely tied to the seacoast, because most of their food came from the ocean. They built seaworthy canoes to fish for salmon and trap lobsters, and to travel the lakes and inland rivers that crisscross the land. Each river was home to a distinct community that had its own Medicine People, artisans, canoe makers, and fishers.

Tidal rivers in Nova Scotia run in every direction since the coastline nearly encircles the province. Rivers flow inland as the tide rises and then change course as the tide falls. The Mi'kmaq understanding of the tides meant that when they were traveling, they could tell how close they were to the sea due to the direction of the river's flow. Therefore, they could plan the timing of their trips. Paddling against the current is difficult when the tide flows upriver. They would've had to paddle very hard to make any headway, but if they timed their trip to go with the flow of the tide, paddling would've been easy and travel swift.

Birch bark canoe made by Mi'Kmaq in Nova Scotia

 MEET

CURATOR ROGER LEWIS, MI'KMAW, SIPEKNE'KATIK, SHUBENACADIE

Roger Lewis is Curator of Mi'kmaq Cultural Heritage at the Nova Scotia Museum. He works with Mi'kmaw artists and the "living objects" they create: "It is important to remember that the maker's soul breathes within them, making them more than a simple craft." He is also a highly skilled canoeist who knows the ancient waterways and is passing along knowledge of the rivers to a new generation.

The Calusa's Watery World

The Calusa lived surrounded by water—the sea and inland waterways—in what is now called Florida. Water provided the fish and shellfish they ate, and influenced how they built their houses, and how they protected themselves from enemies, especially the Spanish. The Calusa built their watercraft from hollowed-out cypress logs. Using a fixed mast and sails woven from palm fronds, they sailed as far as Cuba to trade. They plied the coast looking for shipwrecked Spanish galleons to salvage. Sometimes they even launched sea attacks on Spanish ships.

A CALUSA SAILOR

The day has come! You rub your eyes as you sit up. You can see the ocean. The house has no walls and sits high up on stilts so that when there is a storm—and there are lots of them—waves won't wash it away. Fair weather means a fine day for sailing.

You join the men on the shore. You try to look brave. Your brother reassures you. "You've watched us many times. Now you're ready to help." He shows you how to load the trade goods—piles of shells—so that they don't shift. Balancing your load in the dugout and how to attach the mast are the lessons you learn today. Though this is hard work, you are proud to be on board.

At last the dugout is ready. The people on shore push it off the sand. It rises and falls with the waves. Soon you are laughing as the sea spray hits your face. A school of dolphins swims beside you. They will keep you company all the way to the island.

☉ ☉ ☉

PROTECTING THE GIFT: When Water Is Harmed

We have worked in many ways to protect our waters and the circle of life connected to it.

The Right to Water

Over the years, many Indigenous people have fought for access to water. The Fort Belknap Indian Reservation along the Milk River in Montana was established in 1888 when American settlers began to move into their country. Ranchers and farmers needed large amounts of water for their cattle and their crops, so they built diversion structures to direct the river water to their ranches and homes. Soon, hardly any water from the Milk River reached the A'aninin and the Nakota people in Fort Belknap.

First the A'aninin and Nakota were forced onto a reservation, and now they had no water. The injustice led to an important court case. The court decided that the reservation had rights to water from the Milk River because they used that water before settlers came. This was an important decision, but the government hasn't always acted when the law was broken. Indigenous people have been to court many times since to defend our water rights.

Milk River, at the Montana/Alberta border

WATER-BRINGER WILMA MANKILLER, OKLAHOMA CHEROKEE, 1945–2010

In 1981 Bell, Oklahoma, was a small community with big problems: high unemployment and drug and alcohol abuse. Wilma Mankiller was the director of the Cherokee Nation's Community Development Department. She went to Bell and called a meeting to find out what people wanted most for their community, but they were so disheartened that only one person showed up. For a long time Wilma kept reminding people of the Cherokee principle of *gadugi*, "working together for the community."

The people of Bell said that what they wanted most was running water. Wilma and the community made a plan. They would use federal funds to buy the necessary equipment, and the people would lay the waterline themselves. Using dynamite to blast through rocks and plenty of manual labor to dig the trench, the people of Bell laid 26 kilometers (16 miles) of waterline. The result: clean drinking water and indoor plumbing, and a reignited spirit of *gadugi*.

Wilma Mankiller became the first woman Chief of the Cherokee Nation. When she died in 2010, Indigenous leaders from twenty-three countries lit fires to light her way home.

When Water Is Dammed

In the 1930s the desire for electricity (electricity was relatively new and one-third of the population had none), the desperate need for jobs during the Great Depression, and the fear of floods led the United States government to start building dams. Every dam brought jobs and electricity to the local citizens, but often at a high cost to Indigenous people. The dams flooded the land, destroyed ancient waterways, and flooded the graves of our ancestors.

The dams were also disastrous for other living beings. In 1811 fur trader and mapmaker David Thompson watched the first-salmon ceremony at Kettle Creek in the state of Washington. He wrote that the streams teemed with fish. The

Protesters march through downtown Toronto during the Global Climate Strike.

In a photograph dated August 20, 2019, Norm Moonias heads to the reverse osmosis water shed with nine jugs to fill for the nine people who live at his home in the Neskantaga First Nation in Northwestern Ontario. The community has been under a boil water advisory for over twenty years.

fishing didn't start until well into the salmon run. Then a single fisher with a spear pulled out a limited number of salmon. By 1940 that same first-salmon ceremony was a bittersweet memory, because the Grand Coulee Dam on the Columbia River had changed the course of the river. Salmon had no way to reach their spawning streams. Most of them couldn't return to the streams they sought. Soon there were no more salmon.

Don't Drink the Water!

Canada has the world's third largest amount of fresh water per person. However, for too many Indigenous people in remote communities, water warnings, or advisories, are part of daily life. Grassy Narrows is an Anishinaabe community in northwestern Ontario that lives with a water warning that began fifty years ago.

WATER HERO GEORGE HERON, SENECA, 1919–2011

The first battle against dams took place on the lands of the Seneca Nation. George Heron had served courageously with the U.S. Navy in the South Pacific during World War II. When he returned home, he walked into the Allegheny River to let it wash away any hate he had brought home from war.

His battles weren't over. One of the toughest would happen while he was serving his two terms as Chief. He fought against the Kinzua Dam.

Since 1794 members of the Seneca Nation lived on the Allegany Reservation and the adjacent Cornplanter Tract, which consisted of 12,100 hectares (30,000 acres) in southwestern New York and northwestern Pennsylvania. George Washington's agents signed the U.S. government's pledge that the land belonged to the Seneca in the Treaty of Canandaigua. It said, "The United States will never . . . disturb the Seneka [*sic*] nation, nor any of the Six Nations, or of their Indian friends residing thereon."

A century and a half later, the government did indeed disturb the people. It decided to build the Kinzua Dam across the Allegheny River to control flooding and to generate hydroelectricity. Reservation land would be flooded.

George Heron proposed another site that would leave their land dry; he took the government to court; he lobbied Congress. He didn't succeed. In 1965 the Seneca's homes were bulldozed or burned, and they were moved to new villages on the New York side.

Though the Kinzua Dam was built, the work of George Heron, the Seneca people, and their supporters is a model to follow when mobilizing those who fight projects that damage water.

Kinzua Dam outflow below the Allegheny Reservoir. The Allegheny River flows from the dam south to Pittsburgh.

Ashley Green, a resident of Shoal Lake #40 First Nation, carries a 20-litre (5-gallon) water container into his home in February 2015. After nearly twenty-five years, the water advisory has recently been lifted.

Their water was polluted by industrial mercury waste from a paper mill. Since mercury can enter the food chain, it also contaminates the fish they eat. Just as the people of Grassy Narrows feel the effects of mercury poisoning, so too does the wildlife in the area. Boil water advisories represent the kind of environmental racism that affects the lands where Indigenous people live.

There are three levels of water warnings. "Boil water" means that people can't use tap water to cook, drink, feed pets, brush their teeth, make ice cubes or soups, wash fruits and vegetables, or make baby formula. "Do not consume" means all of this, plus babies, toddlers, and old people shouldn't even wash in tap water. "Do not use" means don't use tap water at all.

Some water advisories date back decades. If you were a member of Neskantaga First Nation in Northern Ontario, you could be a twenty-five-year-old who has never been able to drink the water that comes from your tap.

One of the places that worked for its right to drinkable water is Shoal Lake, in the southeast corner of Manitoba. Since 1998 Shoal Lake First Nation #40 had been under a boil water advisory. The story starts in the early 1900s. The

Stewart Redsky, former Chief of Shoal Lake #40 First Nation, looks out over the dike that separated contaminated water from fresh water in 2015.

Manitoba capital, Winnipeg, some 140 kilometers (87 miles) away, needed water. When the city sent heavy equipment to build the water system for the city, Shoal Lake residents had to move to a peninsula across the bay. The crews cut a channel to divert tannin-laden, boggy water away from the intake for Winnipeg. The peninsula became an island. Crews used gravel from Shoal Lake's ancestral land to build a dam so Winnipeg's water stayed untainted. On one side, contaminated water flowed to the people of Shoal Lake First Nation #40. On the other side, clean water flowed to Winnipeg.

A running-water system built in the 1990s for the reserve didn't work well. There was an outbreak of cryptosporidiosis (a disease that causes stomach cramps, vomiting, and diarrhea) in 1997.

The people of Shoal Lake First Nation #40 had a solution. They lobbied for an all-weather road, which they called Freedom Road, to link their island with the mainland and make their community more accessible. Their plans included bringing in the materials and equipment to build a treatment plant so people can have clean water to drink. These plans of action have resulted in the water advisory being lifted.

THE PERSONHOOD OF WATER

Indigenous people protecting their right to keep Lake Erie free from pollution were joined by their allies from Toledo, Ohio, to call out the polluters. Together they protested the phosphorus dumped into the lake in 2014, which led to the shutdown of the water supply for nearly half a million people. It was an urgent reminder that everyone needs healthy water.

WATER PROTECTOR AUTUMN PELTIER, ANISHINAABE KWE, WIKWEMIKONG UNCEDED TERRITORY

Autumn is from Manitoulin Island in Lake Huron, one of the world's largest bodies of fresh water. She was just eight years old when she first took part in water ceremonies on the lands of the Wikwemikong First Nation. Autumn follows in the footsteps of her auntie, Water Walker Josephine Mandamin, who walked around the Great Lakes bringing the message "The water is sick, and people need to fight for the water."

Autumn first came to the attention of the public at a meeting of the Assembly of First Nations when she gave Canadian Prime Minister Justin Trudeau a copper water pot and challenged him to protect the waters. Since then she has talked about water issues at many international events, including the Children's Climate Conference in Sweden and at the United Nations. In 2017, 2018, and 2019, she was nominated for an International Children's Peace Prize and was named to the United States Union of Concerned Scientists list of 2019 Science Defenders. Her message: "Warrior up!" to protect water.

The late Josephine Mandamin's legacy and work are being continued by her great-niece Autumn Peltier.

Despite a big oil company spending over US$300,000 to influence voters against it, in February 2019 Toledo passed the Lake Erie Bill of Rights, giving Lake Erie personhood. This means that all the citizens of Toledo can act as legal guardians to the lake. They now have the power to sue those who harm or pollute its water.

We remember the story of Beaver and how water links us all. We respect water as sacred. We fight to protect the gift of water from harm, and in places like Toledo, we work with concerned allies to make sure everyone has clean water. Indigenous knowledge about water is only one of the sacred elements of nature.

Another is fire. Joe Gilchrist (Secwepemc Nation and Nlaka'pamux Nation) and Harry Spahan (Coldwater First Nation) are Fire-Keepers in British Columbia. They say, "Fire use by Indigenous peoples was so prevalent across Turtle Island [the name that many Indigenous people use for what we now call North America] that the plant life evolved needing fire. Over the ages, cultural burning on the homelands shaped the lives of humans, plants, animals, and Mother Earth herself. Consider fire as a cleanser, like water but for Mother Earth."

Fire and Smoke Knowledge

Fire and smoke are great gifts. In our most sacred ceremonies, smoke connects our breath with the heavens. Fire cooks our food, helps grow our crops, and even keeps our waters clean. It is a constant reminder of how every being is connected. We know that fires can destroy, but they can also be part of the cycle of life. One example is the way that lodgepole pine trees depend on fire to reproduce.

Lodgepole pines have cones in which the seeds are held by resin. They lie dormant on the forest floor until a fire burns off the resin. After the fire passes and rain falls, millions of seedlings will grow out of the ash and soil.

FIRE-KEEPERS

Fire is powerful. That's why it must never be used without special training from Elders, Fire-Keepers, and Fire Knowledge Holders.

Anyone can set wood ablaze, but becoming a Fire-Keeper takes years of training and supervision to ensure the wise use of fire. Such individuals practice their traditional fire stewardship roles for the benefit of their communities. A Fire-Keeper may be a community member tasked with lighting a fire and keeping it lit for cultural purposes.

Each Indigenous community has its own practices around fire. Every summer, when

my Piikani ancestors traveled, each family appointed a Fire-Keeper. That person carried a smoldering coal in a special horn filled with dried plants from one camp to another. At the new campsite, the Fire-Keeper would kindle a new fire from that coal. Once the women pitched their tipis, they would kindle their campfires from the Fire-Keeper's coal. That way, their new home fires were connected to previous camps. When an Elder held a medicine ceremony, a new sacred fire was started using the powder from dried tree bracket fungus.

Apache woman dances beside a bonfire at a Sunrise Dance on the San Carlos Reservation in Arizona.

Our planet is facing disastrous wildfires caused in part by climate change. Today, our fire knowledge can benefit everyone.

There's a playful Naapi story that reminds us to be watchful around fire.

Naapi Gets Reckless with Fire

Once Naapi was traveling around when he came upon a solitary lodge. He did not know the tipi belonged to the Chief of Fire and his wife. Naapi looked in and saw plenty of dried meat piled inside. As he looked further, he saw some rawhide leggings decorated with feathers hanging from a lodgepole. He immediately wanted them. Suddenly the owner spoke up and invited Naapi to enter the tipi. Naapi stepped inside. After some time, he asked if he could have the leggings. His host, the Chief of Fire, replied that he would not give away those leggings.

As the day was late, Naapi asked if he could sleep in their tipi that night. "Well, my friend, you may sleep here tonight," came the reply. Naapi thought this was wonderful. He had to have those leggings, even if he had to steal them.

Deep in the night when all was quiet, Naapi removed the leggings from their perch and strapped them to his back. He crept out of the tipi and set off. He ran for a long time until he was sure they could not catch him. All the exertion made him tired, so he sat down to rest. He got comfortable and nodded off. When he woke from his slumber, he found himself back in the tipi he had just fled.

Naapi saw the Chief of Fire looking at him and he quickly explained, "Oh! I needed a pillow last night, so I used your leggings." He returned the leggings to the true owner.

His host said, "My friend, join me and we will eat the food my wife cooked."

Naapi ate the meal and spent the day in the tipi. As night fell, he pretended once again to fall asleep. When all was quiet, he stole those leggings. Once again, he strapped them to his back and ran. He was far away from the camp when he grew exhausted. He decided to sit and rest briefly, but he fell asleep instead. When he opened his eyes, he found himself back in the tipi with the leggings strapped to his back. "Maybe your leggings like me and so they keep attaching themselves to me," he mused as he replaced them on the lodgepole. Then he sat down with his host to enjoy a meal.

Naapi tried the same trick that third night only to wake up back in the lodge with the leggings strapped to his back. He was certain that his host was getting suspicious that those leggings were not moving on their own.

Naapi tried once more on the fourth night to sneak off with the leggings, only when he woke up again, he was back in the same tipi. And he had run out of explanations. After they had eaten some food the Chief of Fire said to Naapi, "My friend, those leggings must really like you, so I will give them to you. They are not ordinary leggings, because they carry the power to start fires. I use them when I go hunting and you can do so, too. When you are sure you have game in the brush, put on the leggings and run around. Wherever you step the grass will catch fire. However, I must warn you not to wear them every day. You must only use them for hunting."

Naapi agreed and took the leggings with him. Since he did not steal them this time, he did not wake up back in the lodge of the Chief of Fire. Once he arrived at the camp of his people, he used the leggings when he went hunting and he always returned successful. Naapi noticed that people admired him, so he thought that he might acknowledge all the attention he got by dressing up most fine. He put on the leggings and stepped out to show off his new look. However, everything went bad right away. Wherever he stepped he set the grass ablaze. He ran faster but the fire just spread with him. People in the camp started to panic and run around in distress. They called for Naapi to stop the burning. Finally he stopped and pulled the leggings off him and threw them on the ground where they burned until they were ashes.

This story reminds us that fire is a powerful natural force that is useful for hunting, but it has to be respected.

SACRED SMOKE AND FIRE

Because smoke connects human breath and the spirit world, it is an important part of our sacred practices including smudging, use of the pipe, and our ceremonies.

Smudging

Smudging is a sacred ceremony that cleans our souls of negative thoughts. Each nation has its own private smudging practices, but four of the elements that appear almost everywhere are a container (often a shell) representing water; the four sacred plants that are gifts of Mother Earth (cedar, sage, sweetgrass, tobacco); the fire that's produced from lighting the sacred plants; and the smoke produced from the fire.

During public smudges, the Elder leading the ceremony places a small amount of plant leaves and stems in a shell container. The dried herbs are lit with a wooden match and burn until the flames die out. As smoke rises from the ashes, the Elder invites those in attendance to waft the smoke over themselves. Using their hand or an eagle feather, the person being smudged pulls the smoke to them

Cedar

Sage

Sweetgrass

Tobacco

and gently inhales to keep peace in the mind, heart, and body. Private prayers accompany the burning of sweetgrass, or other plants, for personal smudging.

Smudging is so important that it is included as a healing practice in the Calls to Action from the Truth and Reconciliation Commission of Canada. Although smoke is strictly forbidden in public buildings, many hospitals, including those that are part of the University Health Network in Toronto, have set aside special areas for smudging.

Linda Soriano of the Lummi Nation performs a smudging ceremony at Saint Mark's Episcopal Cathedral in Seattle, fanning smoke from burning sage with eagle feathers onto a totem pole.

TRUTH AND RECONCILIATION

Between 1879 and 1996, the Government of Canada took First Nations, Métis, and Inuit children away from their families and homes and put them in residential schools, where they were not allowed to speak their own language or practice their culture. Children were treated cruelly. Being kept away from their people caused them and their families great sorrow. As part of a settlement for a class action lawsuit in 2008 the Government of Canada created the Truth and Reconciliation Commission (TRC). When it released its final report in 2015, the TRC issued ninety-four Calls to Action. These are actions all governments, courts, businesses, schools, and citizens of Canada can do to help repair the mistakes of the past.

Thousands marched through Ottawa in a rally, led by Indigenous leaders, in memory of the children who died in residential schools.

MEET CLAYTON SHIRT, SADDLE LAKE CREE, TREATY 6, POTAWATOMI

Clayton Shirt is a traditional teacher and healer. He works to help all people "walk in a good way" through life. He is helping to share smudging as a healing practice. He describes the sweetgrass used in smudging as a reminder of the sweetness of life, and the tobacco as a link to the past because in traditional stories, it is one of the first gifts given to people.

He has supported the spiritual, emotional, and knowledge journeys of students and health researchers at the Waakebiness-Bryce Institute for Indigenous Health at the University of Toronto and has performed the smudging ceremony for cancer patients, doctors, and nurses.

Sacred Pipes

Long before my ancestors grew tobacco, they collected a plant called bearberry and mixed it with the inner bark of the red osier dogwood for use in sacred pipes. The smoke was said to carry their prayers to the spirit world.

The oldest pipe we know of was found by archaeologists at an excavation at the Cactus Flower site near Medicine Hat, Alberta. It was probably made five thousand years ago. That was four thousand years before they grew their first tobacco plants.

TOBACCO

Indigenous people consider tobacco to be a sacred plant. Hunters offer tobacco before and after a kill to give thanks to the Creator and to the animal. We spread it on the ground as an offering to the earth and on the water as respect for the gifts it gives us. The tobacco we use in sacred practices is the plant that comes straight from the ground. It isn't treated with the harmful chemicals found in cigarettes. We can't stress this enough: don't confuse sacred tobacco use with the dangerous, health-destroying practice of smoking cigarettes, cigars, regular pipes, or chewing tobacco.

My Piikani ancestors cultivated tobacco at the northern limit of where it could grow. (Farther north, there aren't enough frost-free days.) We tell stories about the Chief of the Beaver giving us knowledge about tobacco. And for good reasons. Beaver dams created an excellent microclimate that protected the young seedlings from late frost. During the dry summer the ponds kept the soil moist for the tobacco roots.

On the Plains, people made pipes of black soapstone or a white or green cupric pipestone. A wooden pipestem that was fitted into the stone bowl drew out the smoke. Pipestems were decorated with feathers, fur, quills, and later with beadwork—decorations that had special meaning for the pipe's owner. Today, we use pipes in prayer or when we have religious ceremonies. Many pipes owners are members of a medicine society or a ceremonial organization. In the past pipes were sometimes called "peace pipes" because smoking together was a sign of sincerity for negotiations between nations.

A Sacred Ceremony: The Fire Dance

Indigenous people often begin their ceremonies with a sacred fire. The Navajo Mountainway ceremony takes place over nine days at the end of winter, and consists of four ceremonies marked by songs and stories. The Fire Dance is performed during the last night, beginning with the lighting of a central bonfire.

THE FIRE DANCE IN NAVAJO

Night has fallen, and the sky is bright with stars. You squeeze past hundreds of people so that you can get to the sacred enclosure in time to see the huge central fire lit. Its flames will burn away all evil.

This is the ninth night of the Mountainway. You are exhausted after all the excitement of watching so many dances and ceremonies. Your grandfather has told you about the Fire Dance, but you've always fallen asleep in your father's arms before it began. Now that you are older you are determined to stay awake.

Finally, in the time just before dawn, the ceremony begins. The central fire has been reduced to embers. Young men drag in trees to feed it. Solemn Medicine Men, specially invited from far away, begin to move in time to the drums. You watch in awe as the flames crackle and soar. Their Fire Dance will give strength to everybody at the gathering. It will make the soil fertile and the animals plentiful. You are grateful that the Fire Dance will bring good crops and game to hunt.

Navajo Fire Dance, by Beatien Yazz (1928-2013)

⊙ ⊙ ⊙

FIRE AND SMOKE KNOW-HOW

Our knowledge of fire and smoke helps us in many practical ways. On the Great Plains where people lived in tipis, the interior of the finished tipi was smoked so that the buffalo skin walls wouldn't harden or leak when it rained. People almost everywhere in North America preferred cooked food and used fire in different ways to prepare it. Indigenous Fire-Keepers knew how to use fire to put nutrients back into the soil, and even to change the landscape.

A Cree woman, Elizabeth Brien, preparing to smoke whitefish on racks at a camp in Quebec in 1988

Cooking with Fire

North America's Indigenous menu is a long one. Whether it's delicate fish, hearty game stews, or sweet fruit and nut puddings, from earliest times Indigenous people have used fire for cooking. Meat might be roasted on a spit over fire. Soup was made in clay pots placed on an open fire. Soup was also made in a wooden bowl that was filled with water first, and then meat, berries, and hot pebbles were added until the water boiled. Vegetables were roasted using an earth oven. People first dug

The Rampanen family demonstrates the ancient art of pit cooking, in Port Alberni, British Columbia.

40

a hole in the ground. They gathered cobbles (rocks that are bigger than pebbles but smaller than boulders) and piled them with wood that was set ablaze. When the fire had made the rocks red-hot, they were removed with a wooden rake and placed at the bottom of the pit. Next, leaves and grasses were placed over them, then all the food was placed atop the leaves. A hollow reed was set in the center, and another layer of plants was placed over the food. Finally, the whole pile was covered with earth. Periodically water could be added through the reed, creating steam from the hot rocks to help cook the food. When the earth around the oven was hot, the embers and ashes were brushed aside. Then the cooked meat and vegetables, like corn, turnips, or other tubers, were removed and ready to eat.

Controlled Burns

Controlled burns—setting carefully planned fires at times when there is little risk to people—are one of the important ways we use fire.

Prescribed burns get rid of built-up "fuel" like pine needles, dead leaves, grasses, twigs, and fallen trees.

Cultural burns are used to benefit the land. They create space for plant diversity and new habitat for wildlife.

Together, these practices reduce the risk of catastrophic wildfires.

Amy Cardinal Christianson (Métis Nation of Alberta) is a fire research scientist with the Canadian Forest Service. She teaches people about cultural burning as a way to keep forests healthy. They are ignited during low-risk conditions, usually early spring or late fall when everything is damp. The fires are low intensity and move slowly through the understory (the plant life underneath the forest canopy). Cultural fires are carried out by experienced people who know what they are doing. For example, a Peavine Métis Settlement tribal Elder once told her that he knew exactly when to burn by examining whether spruce needles on trees were dry.

Amy Cardinal Christianson with her daughter on a spring burn on Treaty 6 territory.

Other cultural burns may be used to protect a species that's especially important to the members of the nation. For instance, a fishing nation might burn riverbank brush to improve the river's quality by clearing away plants that clog it. A hunting nation that relies on moose or deer meat might use a burn to cut down the habitat of ticks that torment the animals, to open trails for the animals, or to spur new grass growth for game to eat.

When settlers came to the Great Plains and saw that we set fires deliberately, they were horrified. They called our fires "deplorable" and our reasons for setting fires "trivial" and "mischievous." Our reasons were not at all "trivial" or "mischievous."

For my Blackfoot buffalo-hunting ancestors, fire was an important tool. (As the people traveled across burned-out areas the ashes made their moccasins and feet turn black, the origin of the name Blackfoot.)

Buffalo look for grazing land with lots of green grass. In the autumn, when the grass turned yellow and was dry and easy to burn, young men went to the places where they planned to hunt buffalo the following spring. They burned the grass above the cliff, knowing that the grass seeds would fall to the ground. The ashes from the burnt grass sank into the earth and made fertilizer for the seeds. The winter snow covered the earth and seeds. Once spring came, the snow melted and added moisture to the thawing soil. This made the grass grow fast and early. Buffalo herds would gather there to graze on the new grass, giving the first hunt after winter the best chance for success.

Yukon First Nations Wildfire plays a key role in protecting forests in the North and training the next generation of firefighters.

WATER AND FIRE: Where's the Connection?

The connection between fire and water isn't just that fire can heat water and water can put out fire. Fires can increase water in forests.

Trees have deep roots that absorb a lot of water. They don't use it all. Some of that water is released into the air as water vapor through tiny pores in their leaves.

Measuring water vapor released from burned patches of forest demonstrates how fires reduce green leaf cover that shades other plants. Fires open the forest canopy and bring in sunlight, which promotes new plant growth and keeps the soil moisture higher than in unburnt forests.

Controlled fires clear out many young trees and underbrush. This leaves fewer plants to pull water from the soil, so more water filters into rivers and reservoirs downstream. There will also be more water for the larger trees that survive the fires. With less competition from other plants, these trees can grow, strengthen, and stay healthy.

Controlled fires make soil more productive because after a fire there is room for new growth. Nutrients added to the soil give young plants the essential minerals they need to thrive. The result? Flourishing berries, medicinal plants, and plants used for basketry.

FIRE WISDOMS, BRAIDED TOGETHER

Today Knowledge Keepers form partnerships with firefighters, government agencies, and volunteer groups to braid together traditional knowledge of fire and new technology. For instance, in Northern California, where annual fires cause great damage and loss of life, the Karuk Tribe has a 232-page plan that calls for prescribed burning to reduce the wildfires that threaten the area.

"Beat the Heat"

Yukon First Nations Wildfire (YFNW) is a partnership created in 2019 by eight Yukon First Nations. YFNW runs "Beat the Heat" Boot Camp, training First Nations youth to be firefighters every season. The participants go through grueling physical training and learn skills that range from how to use firefighting equipment to managing prescribed burns. YFNW takes pride in hiring and training First Nations youth.

In July 2018, YFNW's firefighters were the first on the scene when Tahltan First Nation was devastated by a terrible wildland fire.

The Indigenous Peoples Burning Network

Elizabeth Azzuz (Yurok, Karuk) lives in the Yurok village of Weitchpec, California. She is a leader in the Indigenous Peoples Burning Network (IPBN) in partnership with the government and with the Nature Conservancy. For over fifty years she has used her knowledge of cultural burns to encourage the growth of plants used for traditional weaving and the production of traditional foods, as well as to open meadows for elk and deer. Elizabeth says, "Fire provides open meadows so kids can run and play, so elk can move through historic corridors, and to make room for the hazel we use to weave the baskets our women are renowned for."

Elizabeth Azzuz (Yurok, Karuk)

The Apache 8

Around 14,000 members of the White Mountain Apache Tribe live in eastern Arizona on a reservation of 650,000 spectacular hectares (1.6 million acres) of sparkling rivers, deep forests, and high mountains. The mountains, the trees, the wind, and the clouds are all held to be sacred.

In 2002, over 113,000 hectares (280,000 acres) of the White Mountain Apache Reservation's forest burned. The Apache 8 were among those who fought the fires.

The Apache 8 is a tough, courageous team of Apache women firefighters. When they are not fighting fires, they do the important work of thinning out under-brush in the spring to reduce fuel that might feed an uncontrolled wildfire. They are always on the watch for lightning because when it strikes a tree, a "sleeper" fire can smolder before bursting into flames days later.

From 1974 to 2005, more than one hundred White Mountain Apache women served as wildland firefighters.

Firefighters from Fort Apache conduct a prescribed fire to reduce forest litter buildup.

ABOVE: Butch Gregg and Ericka Hinton on the firefighting crew

LEFT: Wildland firefighters burn warm grass fields to help wildlife.

Our fire knowledge is an important resource that can benefit everyone, especially now that climate change may be a cause of wildfires.

Indigenous knowledge principles guide our actions when we hunt, grow, or fish for our food. Our ideas about conservation practices that help us manage the landscape can benefit the world.

Indigenous Knowledge and Food Security

Sharing and receiving food with family and visitors is an honor. Whether the food is the meat of buffalo, fish, or plants, *Netukulimk* guides us. The Mi'kmaq term *Netukulimk* means "take only what is needed and waste nothing".

THE GIFT OF BUFFALO

My ancestors were among the buffalo hunters of the Great Plains. Buffalo were so important on the Plains that the Lakota called them *Tatanka* or "He who owns us." Our stories remind us of how much we owe to the buffalo.

Buffalo's Gift

One evening a young woman left her family tipi and walked to the river valley to fetch firewood. She saw a buffalo herd grazing in the distance. She could barely remember the taste of buffalo meat because she had not eaten any in such a long time. She had learned to ignore hunger pangs, but the sight of the buffalo was like a flint-tipped arrow stabbing her stomach. "If only they would bring themselves near the edge of the cliff so we could have fresh meat, I would marry the Chief of the herd," she said. The Chief of the Buffalo heard her words. He thought that he might like to be married to this woman.

The next evening when the woman walked to the riverbank to gather wood the Chief of the Buffalo left the herd and transformed himself into a man. He waited on the trail. When she approached he began to sing his courtship song. The song delighted her. He introduced himself as the Chief of the buffalo herd. "I heard your wish. If you marry me, I will make sure that your people never go hungry."

"Is this true?" she asked.

The Buffalo Chief reached into the pouch on his belt. In his palm were two tiny stone buffalo. "These are *iinisskimmiksi*," he said. "They are charms that will help your people when they hunt buffalo. I will teach you a song and show you the ceremony that releases their power. Bring them to a Medicine Man and teach him the song and ceremony."

The story reminds us how closely our lives and the lives of buffalo are entwined. Hunting was the only way to ensure food security, because hunger was always a worry. We were taught to be grateful for the animals' gifts to us. Our duty was to leave enough animals alive to reproduce so that the herds were always replenished.

Every part of the buffalo my ancestors hunted had a purpose. After the animals were

Buffalo stones, or *iinisskimmiksi*, form when cycles of freezing and thawing break apart ammonite shells and leave behind a fossil that looks like a small stone buffalo. Medicine Men often used an *iinisskimm* in sacred practices for summoning buffalo.

She thought about her starving family and took the *iinisskimmiksi*. She would marry the Chief of the Buffalo so the people would never know hunger again.

When she got home, she set the wood by her tipi. Her father was a Medicine Man and she taught him the words and the ceremony. He pounded his drum and sang four rounds of the song. He performed each step of the ceremony as his daughter instructed.

As he completed it all, there was the sound of a great thunder. The ground trembled as if a thousand pounding hooves were galloping. When morning dawned, the people found a large herd of buffalo had run over the cliff. They took their flint knives and butchered the animals.

The young woman remembered her promise. She picked up her clay pots as if she were going to the river for water. The others were busy peeling hides and cutting up meat. They didn't notice when she disappeared. A young man was waiting for her on the trail. He transformed her into a buffalo and brought her back to the herd with him.

Many seasons later she visited her father in a dream. She told him that she had not died. She was living with the buffalo. Some of the animals they hunted were her children. Ever after, the people observed the *iinisskimm* ritual before the hunt. They remembered her sacrifice and made sure to offer their respect for the gift of the buffalo after the hunt was over.

Untitled (Buffalo Spirit)
by Garnet Tobacco (Cree)

killed, the hides were removed to use for clothing, moccasins, drums, cradles, and toys. The meat was cut into pieces and divided up. Because we killed dozens of animals at the same time, there was too much meat to eat at once, so most of it was wind-dried. Then it is pounded to a powder to make pemmican, which was a mixture of dried meat, crushed berries, and grease from marrow fat. It lasted for months and was stored in rawhide bags. Pemmican has become a popular dish for long-distance runners because it is a protein-rich food that tastes good, too.

Buffalo bones were turned into clubs, knives, and digging tools. The horns made good cups and fire carriers. The sinews were used as thread to sew clothes and shelters, the tail for brushes, and the chips for fuel. The remaining meat and bones were left behind for bears, wolves, wolverines, coyotes, and birds. In this way other creatures could benefit from the bounty of the hunt.

Buffalo Heroes: The People of Fort Peck

Giving back is part of Indigenous knowledge. The Assiniboine and Sioux Tribes on the Fort Peck Reservation of Montana are repaying the gift of the buffalo by helping to restore them to the Great Plains.

No one knows how many buffalo once lived on the open prairie. Estimates run as high as 60 million. We do know that they were hunted nearly to extinction by 1880. The U.S. government wanted our land for settlers, but we were in the way. When the railroad was built across the Plains, hunters with rifles were encouraged to shoot buffalo from the train cars because once the buffalo were gone, the Indigenous people who depended on them would be starved out of existence. By 1900 fewer than three hundred buffalo were left in the United States. All the buffalo in the world today are descended from those animals.

The people of the Fort Peck Reservation were the first to fight to restore the buffalo. Twenty-three animals living in a remote valley of Yellowstone National

A buffalo is released from a quarantine trailer after being relocated to the Fort Peck Indian Reservation, Montana, in 2019.

Park had survived. Working with Defenders of Wildlife for six years, Fort Peck fought the Government of Montana to get the descendants of those animals.

The first Yellowstone buffalo—around sixty of them—finally arrived at Fort Peck in 2012 and were welcomed with a special ceremony. There are now more than 375 buffalo at Fort Peck in what is the single largest conservation herd. Robbie Magnan is the buffalo manager. As the big horse trailers carrying the buffalo arrived at Fort Peck, he said, "They are coming home to our people!"

First Nations women preparing a buffalo hide in Rossburn, Manitoba

Today, many others, including the Blood Nation in southern Alberta, are fighting to save the buffalo. In 2014, thirteen tribal nations from Canada and the U.S. signed a Buffalo Treaty outlining the importance of bringing back free-roaming buffalo. Now the herd on the prairies is four thousand animals strong.

THE GIFT OF SALMON

"The salmon was put here by the Creator for our use as part of the cycle of life. It gave to us, and we, in turn, gave back to it through our ceremonies . . . Their returning meant our continuance was assured because the salmon gave up their lives for us. In turn, when we die and go back to the earth, we are providing that nourishment back to the soil, back to the riverbeds, and back into that cycle of life."

—Carla HighEagle, Nez Perce, Lapwai

Nations on both the East and West coasts have sacred ceremonies honoring the salmon and ways of fishing that ensure there will be salmon for future generations.

Sacred Salmon

Indigenous people of the West Coast greet the annual salmon migration with great joy because the fish bring food security. They appoint a salmon Chief for the tribe and he selects a fisher for the honor of catching the first salmon of the year. Before entering the river, the fisher is blessed. Once a fish is caught, it is brought to shore and carefully cooked and shared with everyone. The head of the fish is kept pointed upriver to show the salmon's spirit the way home. The bones are cleaned and returned to the river so that salmon can complete their journey and continue to feed the people.

Sts'ailes first-salmon ceremonies honor the current returning salmon as they have done for countless generations, which involves putting the bones and unused portions of the first salmon back in the river.

Traditional Salmon-Fishing Ways

Mature Pacific salmon return from the ocean to spawn in the same stream where they were born. At the mouths of rivers, the salmon mill about until they undergo a metamorphosis, or a change in their form, so that they can swim in freshwater streams once they leave the salty ocean. Indigenous people built stone fish traps in the tidal zone at the mouths of some streams. When the tide was falling and they had caught enough fish, they opened gates to release the rest.

Once the salmon complete their change, they leave the ocean and begin their journey to the streams where they were born, and there they will spawn and die. As they decompose, their bodies provide essential nutrients that help river ecosystems thrive. Indigenous fishers waited for several days before the fishing started. They didn't take the first fish and they didn't take the last. They were careful to let the best salmon through so they could reach the spawning streams and reproduce. And when there was enough to eat and plenty of smoked salmon to last all winter, the fishing stopped.

Archaeologists excavate at Smokehouse Island, as part of a community-engaged collaboration between the Lake Babine Nation and the University of Northern British Columbia.

SMOKEHOUSE ISLAND

Around one thousand years ago, the ancestors of the Babine people in northern British Columbia used wood and stone tools to build an artificial island at the mouth where the Babine River flows out of Babine Lake to the Pacific Ocean. This amazing engineering feat channeled returning salmon into one arm of the river where the community built a fishing weir—a type of fence set in the water to trap fish. Smokehouse Island is still used today for fishing and to smoke salmon, preserving them for the winter food supply, just like their ancestors.

Defenders of the Salmon: Fort Folly First Nation

The Bay of Fundy lies between Nova Scotia and New Brunswick. It is the home of the Inner Bay of Fundy Atlantic salmon, one of the most endangered species in eastern North America.

The Inner Bay of Fundy Atlantic salmon spend their early years in freshwater streams. Like Pacific salmon they swim to the ocean to finish growing into adults, but Atlantic salmon do not spawn and die. Once they mature they return to the rivers where they were born. There they spawn and then they return to the sea until the next season. One adult will repeat this cycle several times in its lifetime.

Once there were thousands of Inner Bay of Fundy salmon. Nobody is sure why, but in recent years fewer than two hundred salmon have been returning to the rivers. In 2003 this species was listed as endangered under Canada's Species at Risk Act.

The Mi'kmaq from Fort Folly are partnering with scientists and universities to save the Inner Bay of Fundy salmon. Once the fry grow to be young salmon (smolts), people from Fort Folly help retrieve them from Fundy National Park rivers and the Petitcodiac watershed. They take the smolts to the world's first wild salmon marine conservation farm on Grand Manan Island in the Bay of Fundy. When they are ready to spawn, they are released back into the rivers where they were born.

The hope is that the fish will produce enough offspring to jump-start the wild population. Though the numbers are still uncertain, the long-term plan is to increase the number of healthy fish.

Wild endangered Atlantic salmon are grown to maturity on the world's first wild salmon marine conservation farm at Dark Harbour on Grand Manan Island, New Brunswick.

THE SWINOMISH: People of the Salmon

The Swinomish in Washington call themselves the People of the Salmon. When fishing season starts in May everyone gathers on the beach for a first-salmon ceremony. It ends when a boat takes one salmon north, another east, another west, and another south. The fish are eased into the water with a prayer that they will tell the other salmon how well they were treated.

Salmon season used to last until December. Now it is only a few days long. There are many reasons for this, especially the impact of climate change. Rivers in which the salmon spawn are getting warmer; ocean acidification is disrupting the food chain (the oceans absorb about one-third of the carbon dioxide from cars, planes, and factories) and damaging sea life by eroding the shells of clams, oysters, and urchins; and, there are more destructive storms.

The Swinomish people recognize the impact of climate change and are working to give back to the salmon and other living beings. They are restoring the intertidal lands and channels that salmon use. Cold, clean waters are essential for spawning salmon, so the people are planting trees along streambeds to cool waters and reduce heat stress on the fish.

They are also restoring oyster reefs, planning the first modern clam garden in the United States, and using remote cameras to monitor elk and deer so that they know how many animals can be hunted without the danger of taking too many. And they are preserving native plants that help naturally manage coastal flooding by stabilizing the foreshore environment, the part of the shore between high- and low-water marks.

Looking across Swinomish Channel from La Conner, Washington, to the fishing port on the Swinomish Reservation.

CLAM GARDENS

The Coast Salish people in British Columbia believed that a human girl was clam digging when she didn't notice that the tide was coming in. The seas closed over her. She became the Maiden of the Seas, a spirit being who warns fishers of danger—a reminder to respect the power of the ocean.

For thousands of years shellfish have been an essential part of the diet for many coastal people, from the Squamish in Vancouver, to the Tlingit on the islands and coast of southern Alaska, and Inuit of Qikiqtarjuaq on Baffin Island. Clams are a delicious source of protein and healthful minerals whether they are eaten raw, boiled, baked, fried in fish oil, steamed, roasted, added to soup, or dried.

Coastal people shaped the clam shells into spoons and ladles, or cups for sipping soup. Artists used the sharp edges of the shells to carve jewelry and glass.

A member from the Coast Salish displays bundles of Manila clams in Buckley Bay on Vancouver Island, British Columbia.

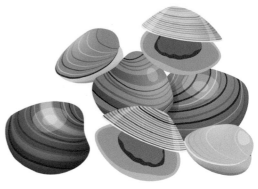

Indigenous people observed the environment that mollusks preferred. Then they built artificial clam gardens that mimicked those conditions. They made rock walls at the low tide line along the edges of bays and inlets to expand the area where clams could thrive. They learned when to thin out the numbers so that each clam had room to grow and to prevent the clams from catching diseases from one another. They learned when to add to the habitat and how many clams they could harvest while leaving enough for the future. These practices were so successful that some clam gardens are still flourishing, after three thousand years!

Today, reclaiming ancient aquacultural knowledge is an ongoing project for youth who use it with modern research methods. Clam gardens along the shorelines of the W̱SÁNEĆ Territory in British Columbia are thousands of years old. From 2014 to 2019, the W̱SÁNEĆ partnered with Parks Canada in the Clam Garden Restoration Project, which is the first of its kind. W̱SÁNEĆ and Hul'q'umi'num Elders, harvesters, and youth are restoring the habitat for clam gardens by mimicking the conditions preferred by mussels, oysters, littleneck clams, horse clams, and burrowing clams such as the geoduck.

THE GIFT OF PLANTS

Think about how our lives are braided together with plants: Plants and trees need carbon dioxide and they give off oxygen. We breathe in oxygen and breathe out carbon dioxide.

The plants (as well as game, fish, and birds) that grow on our land are called "country food," and many Indigenous people are returning to them.

In the far North, geese, seals, lake trout, blueberries, and cloudberries are just a few country foods. In the Southwest, you might feast on pine nuts, rainbow trout, and turkey. And on the Great Plains, delicious prairie turnip, wild rice, blueberries, and venison might be on the menu. In the eastern woodlands, country foods include all kinds of treats made from maple syrup: maple cakes, maple sugar, and maple taffy. Strawberries were once country foods that farmers domesticated and grew in their gardens. They were called "heart berries" and were held in high esteem because of their flavor.

THE FIRST WILD STRAWBERRY

You feel the damp chill seep through your jeans as you lie on the ground. The winter snows have only just melted, but you are impatient for spring. Gently, you nudge last year's dead grasses aside to look for the first sign of strawberry leaves.

You know the story well. When Sky Woman fell to Earth, she brought strawberries with her. And when her daughter died and a heartbroken Sky Woman buried her child, strawberries grew from the girl's heart. No wonder it is called the "heart berry."

Sky Woman, an oil painting, by Ernest Smith (Seneca), Tonawanda Reservation, 1936

The Elders have taught you that wild strawberries are a gift. Nobody planted them. They are shaped just like tiny hearts, and their roots are long, like veins running through the earth.

Finally, the day comes when you see the first tender leaves, and then the first hard yellow berries. You force yourself to wait until they turn red.

Once the berries are ripe, you pick them carefully and carry them home. Most of the berries will be dried for winter. Your mother will give you berry juice to make you strong. You can't resist eating a handful after you fill your basket. Your grandmother sees your berry-stained mouth, but she doesn't scold. She smiles. "I picked wild strawberries, too."

◉ ◉ ◉

Sts'ailes grandfather and grandson picking blackberries

Harvesting wild plants was not the only way to ensure food security. Our ancestors also learned how to domesticate them and in doing so they discovered farming. Around 12,500 years ago people began to collect the seeds of wild plants and till the soil to make gardens. There are many theories about why our ancestors began to domesticate plants, but we know that people have been growing plants ever since.

At least five thousand years ago the Olmec in Mexico domesticated cotton from a small wild tree or shrub. They harvested the cotton bolls and spun the fibers with spindle whorls. The threads were then woven into fabrics. Indigenous people have always been generous with

THE GIFTS FROM PLANTS

Ancient people used plants for all kinds of purposes. Hundreds of plants were medicines. Plant fibers were woven into nets for fishing, and bottle gourds were used as floats for fishing nets. The sap of the bloodroot, a white flower native to eastern North America, was used as a dye. (In Algonquin communities it was associated with love. Men would wear bloodroot paint when they went courting.)

Seed pods with cotton on a kapok tree, also known as the sacred ceiba tree

Indigenous Tzotzil woman weaving a traditional Huipil at the loom

their knowledge as sharing and adapting are good ideas: not surprisingly, growing cotton and weaving traditions spread northward quickly.

Sometimes people domesticated plants such as gourds to use them as musical instruments, or just because they thought that flowers were beautiful.

And, of course, they grew plants for food. If you enjoy potatoes, tomatoes, chocolate, peanuts, sweet potatoes, sunflowers, peppers, pineapples, avocados, bananas, strawberries, pecans, and jalapeño peppers for spice, remember they are the gifts given to us from the Indigenous farmers and gardeners in North and South America who first grew them.

The Three Sisters

There is evidence from a cave in Oaxaca, Mexico, that people were planting pumpkin-type squashes at least 10,700 years ago. They were planting corn crops in the same area about 7,000 years ago and by 5,000 years ago they were also growing beans in their gardens. Through years of patient watching and experimenting, people learned that these plants grow best when the seeds are sown in the same garden plots. Together, corn, squash, and beans are known as the Three Sisters.

Three Sisters gardens braid together all the principles of Indigenous knowledge: they are held to be sacred; we give thanks with ceremonies such as the

"I love being around art every day," said Shawnee Martinez, a seventeen-year-old high school student, about her summer job, working on the mosiac outside the east building of the Albuquerque Convention Center. The section Shawnee worked on is called "The Three Sisters," referring to corn, beans, and squash. The mosiac woman is Maria Martinez, the famous potter from San Ildefonso Pueblo.

Green Corn Festivals or Busks that take place across North America; and they are examples of connection because they do better when grown together than if they are planted separately.

Knowledge of the Three Sisters is held in the stories of farming cultures. Though each nation has its own way of telling the story, the plants are always women, and they are almost always sisters. One story describes a woman dressed in yellow, with long flowing hair. She has two sisters, one who wears green while the other is clad in orange. In the deepest winter, the three of them take shelter in a dwelling. The local people find them and learn they are facing hardship. Although they have little food, the local people share what they have with the sisters. Later, the sisters reveal their true identities—corn, beans, and squash—and reward the people for their generosity with bundles of seeds so that they will never go hungry.

The Three Sisters method of growing, with beans planted to climb up corn stalks, and squash growing underneath

Stories of the Three Sisters originated in ancient times, but they meant so much that they continued to be cherished, even under terrible circumstances. In 1838 the Cherokee were rounded up and forced off their land in Georgia. In the dead of winter, they were forced to walk all the way to Oklahoma, about 3,200 kilometers (2,000 miles) away. Three thousand died; this tragedy is called the Trail of Tears. A Cherokee version of the Three Sisters story dating from that tragic time describes how three of the women took their knowledge with them so that they could plant corn, squash, and beans when they got to the Oklahoma Territory.

In customary farming practices, corn was planted first. Its white spike turned green almost as soon as the sun touched it. When the corn stalks grew tall, beans were sown at their base. If fast-growing beans were planted alone, they could overrun everything in the garden. But beans and corn together were another story. Beans took their time finding the light because they had enough nourishment from bean seeds, and they added nitrogen to the soil. The corn's sturdy stalk gave tender, climbing bean vines the support they needed as they reached for sunlight. The last "sister" planted was the squash. It suppressed the weeds and its shade kept the soil cool. Besides, deer and other animals didn't like to eat squash, so they tended to stay away from the Three Sisters and their gardens.

THE GIFT OF CORN

There is no such thing as wild corn. It is an example of Indigenous observation and experimenting. Corn has spread to almost every part of North America—and the world—to provide about 21 percent of human nutrition.

Corn was probably bred from teosinte, which looks like a skinny ear of corn with twelve kernels inside, all in a stone-hard casing. A gardener in southern Mexico about nine thousand years ago must have noticed a teosinte plant with kernels that were exposed a bit, or perhaps ears that held together, or more rows of kernels than the others, and crossed it with an ancient kind of maize. Over the next thousand years, hundreds of gardeners watched and experimented to create what we recognize as corn.

SIOUX CHEF SEAN SHERMAN, OGLALA LAKOTA

Sean Sherman calls himself the Sioux Chef. He educates people about Indigenous food that contains ingredients that come from the land. He doesn't use wheat flour, dairy, cane sugar, or beef, pork and chicken. Instead, his recipes call for country foods such as wild manzanita berries and acorns from the West Coast to make puddings, or seaweed from Maine to season Atlantic oysters, or white cedar from Minnesota to add flavor to roast venison. The country foods he uses—prairie turnip, true wild rice, ginger, mustard, sunchoke, blueberries, muskrat, and fish from Lake Superior—are delicious. However, that is not the only reason to eat them. They are packed with vitamins, minerals, and healthy fiber.

He has brought together a team of Anishinaabe, Mdewakanton Dakota, Navajo, Northern Cheyenne, Oglala Lakota, Sisseton Wahpeton Dakota, and a growing network of, as he puts it, adventurers, foragers, and food lovers who are reclaiming the cuisine of their ancestors. They founded the non-profit North American Traditional Indigenous Food Systems to give people the chance to learn about Indigenous cuisine and to start restaurants, catering companies, and food trucks in their tribal communities.

A RECIPE FOR SMART FOOD WAYS

Netukulimk is a Mi'kmaw term of respect for the bounty of nature. It begins with the principle of taking only what is needed and wasting nothing. When you are gathering plants or hunting or fishing, don't take the first that you find in case there are no more. Don't take the last you find so there will be more in the future.

Preserve food diversity. For instance, one of our most valued sources of diversity is our ancient seeds. Once there were many different kinds of seeds—there were many varieties of corn, squash, and beans. Indigenous farmers are rallying to bring back the traditional crops that fed our ancestors, and the seeds they grew, by setting up seed banks and sanctuaries to save seeds.

Respect connections. Remember how we are connected to everything living. For instance, species such as bees, flies, moths, butterflies, wasps, and even hummingbirds and bats pollinate nearly three-quarters of the plants that produce 90 percent of the world's food. Plants keep the pollinators fed. When we take care of the pollinators' environment, we are taking care of our food supply.

MEET ENTOMOLOGIST DR. KYLE BOBIWASH, ANISHINAABE NATION

As a boy, Dr. Bobiwash loved to watch crawling insects and to catch butterflies to see how they behaved. Later, he studied them at university and found his career in entomology (the study of insects). He is now a professor at the University of Manitoba, where his research focuses on understanding the ecology of beneficial insects for agriculture and for the greater landscape.

Indigenous knowledge of water, fire, and food are all links in the circle of health for everything on earth. In the next chapter, we look at health practices—not only for individuals, but also for communities, nations, and the earth itself.

Healing Knowledge Ways

We've always had women and men among us who held the knowledge of plants passed down to them by earlier generations. They knew the plants that make medicines to treat pain, ease upset stomachs, and relieve headaches. They knew how to set broken bones, and archaeologists have found evidence from South and Central America that people practiced trepanation, which is cutting or boring a hole in the skull to relieve migraine pain or to treat other brain disorders.

Common yarrow (*Achillea millefolium*)

This chapter isn't about all these skills or medicines. Rather, it is about the way Indigenous people think about health and healing.

For living things to be healthy, there has to be harmony: harmony between a person's body, mind, and spirit; harmony between individuals; harmony between communities; and harmony with the earth. Indigenous people design their healing practices in order to restore that harmony when it is lost.

Fireweed blooming in the Yukon wilderness

HARMONY WITHIN

The Medicine Wheel and the sweat lodge have been used for centuries, and they still help sick or troubled people.

The Medicine Wheel

A Medicine Wheel, sometimes called the Sacred Hoop, can be a work of art like a painting, or it can be a construction on the land. In either case, the circle is a symbol of continuity, with no beginning or end. The circle represents wholeness, constant movement, and unity.

Medicine Wheels on the landscape were always built at the summit of a knoll, a hill, or a butte that offers a good view right to the horizon. They were stone constructions where spiritual leaders conducted sacred ceremonies, or where individuals went to make an offering, pray, and find healing. They left their troubles behind with their offerings.

Medicine Wheel/Medicine Mountain National Historic Landmark in the Bighorn Mountains of Wyoming

Ancient people built nearly 150 Medicine Wheels across the northern Plains and they all feature a stone circle with spokes connected to a central cairn—a pile of stones. The Majorville Medicine Wheel, near the Blackfoot Reserve south of Bassano, Alberta, includes a central cairn where people piled stones beginning around 5,300 years ago.

The cairn and the surrounding circle are connected by twenty-eight spokes. There are still traces of offerings of sweetgrass, willow, cloth, and tobacco from people who have taken part in healing ceremonies there. There are also *iinisskimmiksi* or buffalo-calling stones, perhaps left by those who visited the Medicine Wheel to pray for a successful buffalo hunt

The Sweat Lodge

My Piikani ancestors used sweat lodges to keep clean, but they also used them as ceremonial spaces. Those of us who take part in the sweat lodge ceremony are renewing our relationship with the medicine bundle at the heart of the sweat. The sweat lodge ceremony cleanses body, mind, and soul to restore balance in our lives.

Piikani sweat lodges are made with willow poles set in a circle. The poles are bent and joined by interweaving them. Buffalo or deer hides cover the frame to create a low, domed structure. Nowadays the sweat lodge still uses willow poles, but it is covered with canvas tarps.

My ancestors made tools from stone, so they knew a lot about different kinds of rocks. They chose igneous cobbles to heat the sweat lodge. This type of stone retains heat and does not break apart when doused with water. We still follow that practice.

Preparing a sweat lodge ceremony begins with a pile of wood set ablaze to heat the stones. The red-hot stones are placed in a small pit dug in the middle of the sweat lodge, and the entrance is closed. Water is poured over the hot rocks to produce steam.

Six to eight men sit in the sweat lodge and sing special songs. Prayers are said and a pipe full of tobacco is passed around. The ceremony is repeated four times. The door is opened between the repetitions so that the heat can escape.

Young Cree man in a sweat lodge, in the Cree Nation of Chisasibi, James Bay, Quebec

SWEAT LODGE KNOWLEDGE KEEPER CRAIG FALCON, BLACKFOOT

Craig Falcon is a cultural education consultant who teaches across North America. Today sweat lodges help heal people in psychological distress. Craig Falcon leads sweat lodges for veterans who struggle to make the change from military to civilian life because of post-traumatic stress disorder (PTSD). He explains, "You come back from war with things attached to you, and some of those things may not be good . . . Ceremonies help wash those things off, send them back to where they came from and get you back to who you are." The U.S. Department of Veterans Affairs has recognized the value of the sweat lodge to Indigenous service members since the 1990s. For instance, the Spokane Veterans Center offers the sweat lodge to Indigenous and non-Indigenous veterans suffering from PTSD.

Restoring Harmony: With Games

Games as medicine? In fact, games like lacrosse and double ball built individual strength and community spirit. They also acted as ceremonial battles to settle disputes and strengthen diplomatic ties, thus restoring harmony between communities. The game of chunkey was probably first played around the 11th century in the city of Cahokia near what is now St. Louis, Missouri, and spread to the East Coast as a way to settle disputes.

Members of First Nations teams compete in the traditional game of lacrosse in Montreal.

PLAYING CHUNKEY

You and your brothers have been arguing with another family about two fast horses. The Elders have had enough. A game of chunkey will settle things before the argument turns violent. You will play against one of your enemies.

A crowd has gathered at the long chunkey alley. The loud betting subsides as you take your place. You hold a notched hickory pole coated in bear oil.

You shift from foot to foot. Your brothers nod encouragement. Your grandfather has the great honor of carrying your town's precious chunkey stone to the alley. Your grandfather hands the stone to you. You hurl it down the alley and the game begins.

You and your opponent sprint down the alley. When you judge the stone is about to come to rest, you both throw your poles. The other man's pole comes to rest closest to the stone, so he gets a point.

You are drenched in sweat by the end. The other man has won with twelve points, but at least the grudge has been settled. You are expected to get along from now on. You are sure that your Elders will see to it that you do!

Chunkey Stone — A.D. 1200/1400
Mississippian Possibly Illinois

⊙ ⊙ ⊙

Another traditional game taught by the Mandan, Arikara and Hidatsa is the arrow toss game, here played on the Fort Berthold Reservation, North Dakota.

Braiding Together Indigenous Healing and Western Science

MEET MEDICINE MAN DR. LINDSAY CROWSHOE, PIIKANI

One of the Calls to Action from the Truth and Reconciliation Commission is for more Indigenous health care workers. Canada's seventeen medical schools are teaming up with the Indigenous Health Network to increase the number of Indigenous students in their programs.

Dr. Crowshoe began his medical career in 1995 after graduating from the University of Alberta Medical School. He now teaches in the Faculty of Medicine at the University of Calgary, where he is the Director of the Indigenous Health Program. He is also a primary care physician for Indigenous people in the city of Calgary.

MEET MEDICINE WOMAN DR. ESTHER TAILFEATHERS, KAINAI

Esther Tailfeathers was born and raised on the Blood Reserve in southern Alberta. At a young age she volunteered as a candy striper in a local hospital. She never let go of her desire to help people who were experiencing poor health. Eventually her interest led her to medical school at the University of North Dakota. Afterward she completed her residency at the University of Alberta hospitals. Since 2000, Dr. Tailfeathers has been the primary care physician for the Blood Tribe. She was a frontline worker mobilizing her community's response to the fentanyl crisis and led the efforts to safeguard health care, especially at the Elders Lodge, during the COVID-19 pandemic. Throughout her medical career she has advocated for better representation of Indigenous people in the health care professions.

HARMONY WITH THE ENVIRONMENT— CARING FOR THE EARTH'S HEALTH

The ideas of Indigenous knowledge can help us protect the environment, especially against the effects of climate change.

Champions for a Healthy Earth

The Tulalip Beaver Project

When beavers build dams, they increase freshwater storage, and that's good for wetland creatures and fish habitat. Beaver dams reduce the effects of increasingly intense storms. They also transform the landscape by increasing grazing opportunities for deer, elk, and other game, and create homes for birds, frogs, and toads.

Tulalip biologists and volunteers weave branches and other vegetation through a framework of vertical posts to construct a beaver dam. They hope that this temporary structure will provide relocated beavers with a home base and a head start as they begin to do their own ecological engineering.

In the 1800s, beavers were trapped to extinction for their fur, but now their numbers are increasing and there are places that need their help. The Tulalip Tribes of Washington are relocating beavers from suburban areas where they are not wanted to areas such as the Snohomish watershed that really need them.

The Southeast Alaska Tribal Toxins (SEATT) Partnership

Phytoplankton are microscopic marine organisms. Many small fish species feed on plankton but so do larger animals such as whales. The Alaska tribes in SEATT are using ultrafine nets, filtering apparatuses, and training resources to collect, identify, and monitor phytoplankton types in the waters off their section of the coast. Their goal is to protect the ocean environment from harmful algal blooms.

Phytoplankton bloom (green and blue swirls) near the Pribilof Islands off the coast of Alaska, in the Bering Sea. The turquoise waters are likely colored by a type of phytoplankton called coccolithophores.

Orcas (killer whales) surface in Lynn Canal, an inlet in Alaska, with a view of the Chilkat Mountains in the distance.

73

For generations, the people of the Lutsel K'e Dene First Nation have depended on their traditional territory for sustenance. The area of Thaidene Nëné supports a way of life.

The Lutsel K'e Dene First Nation

The boreal forest that rings the northern part of the globe is important to every living thing on Earth. Its wetlands, such as bogs, capture carbon dioxide from the atmosphere and store it. Many species of birds nest there and then migrate as far as the southern tip of South America, eating insects and spreading seeds along the way. This vast tract of forest is home to grizzly bears, wolves, birds, fish, and some of the last free-ranging herds of barren-ground caribou. Its rivers bring nutrients to the sea, feeding the fish that feed us. The Lutsel K'e Dene First Nation in the Northwest Territories is one of the leaders in conserving the vital boreal forest.

There are no highways connecting Lutsel K'e to the rest of the Northwest Territories.

The Lutsel K'e Dene First Nation worked in cooperation with Nature United and the Nature Conservancy, Parks Canada, and the Government of Canada to establish the Thaidene Nëné National Park Reserve and Territorial Protected Area and Wildlife Conservation Area. It encompasses 23,376 square kilometers (9,000 square miles) of boreal forest and tundra and supports an ecosystem with some of the cleanest, freshest water in the world.

The Lutsel K'e Dene are the stewards of the park to make sure that visitors treat the water, land, and wildlife with respect. They also run educational programs about conservation and introduce visitors to traditional practices.

CITIZEN SCIENCE!

Anyone can add to our body of knowledge. "Citizen Science" describes people of all ages and all walks of life who work with professional scientists to gather important information. If you want to join them, there are lots of ways to do it. Around the world, there are hundreds of groups of citizen scientists who do vital work: they count bees, fish, and birds; they track butterflies; and they record information about coastlines for many vital projects.

A great example is Wabanaki Youth in Science (WaYS). WaYS started in Maine when the environmental leaders of the nations that make up the Wabanaki ("People of the Dawn") were getting ready to retire. They wanted to ensure that young people could take their place. Students from each of the nations were linked with natural resource staff from their tribe to work on environmental topics, such as counting bugs collected from stream samples—a big part of checking the health of the water.

WaYS interns collecting understory plant data on a milacre plot in a white pine (*Pinus strobus*) plantation degraded by a dense understory of non-native invasive plants such as glossy buckthorn (*Frangula alnus*).

Indigenous knowledge is at the foundation of our healing practices. It is what guides us as we try to restore the health of our bodies, our communities, and the earth.

Our knowledge of the skies—the Sky Wolves' realm—is another way that we apply Indigenous knowledge.

Sky
Knowledge

From ancient times, Indigenous astronomers studied the sun, moon, planets, and stars to give us our maps, our calendars, beliefs about how to govern, and even directions for building our homes.

WAYFINDING

The night sky is a map based on the positions of the moon, the stars, and the planets. People with sky knowledge could travel great distances. My ancestors walked the Old North Trail—one of the oldest and longest roads in the world—to trade, to go on spiritual journeys, or because they were simply curious about what lay over the next hill. They were able to follow a trail that was 3,200 kilometers (2,000 miles) long because they had a mental map of stories they were told, their memories of their own past travels, and a knowledge of the skies.

The Pole Star

My Piikani ancestors thought that the earth was flat and that high above the earth was a flat sky world. The stars were people who traveled through the night, all except for Okiinaa, also known as Polaris, the Pole Star, or the North Star. It is the most important marker in the night sky because unlike the other stars, it doesn't move. Okiinaa's story became part of Blackfoot oral history about 1,500 years ago. We can state this with confidence because modern astronomers agree that is when the earth's axis began to point to Polaris, which became known as the Pole Star.

Ancestors by Brit Ellis/Blue Hummingbird, Haudenosaunee
The artist uses beadwork to honour her Haudenosaunee creation story and her relations and ancestors in Sky World and all the wisdom they carry.

HOW POLARIS BECAME THE POLE STAR

If you can find the Pole Star in the sky, you can orient yourself. Imagine that the earth is a spinning top. Our planet spins around an imaginary line—an axis—that runs through it. If you follow the axis out into space from the Northern Hemisphere where we live, it points right at Polaris, also called the North Star or the Pole Star because it is right above the earth's North Pole.

This wasn't always so, and it won't be so in the future. Okiinaa's story is an accurate oral record of when Polaris became the North Star 1,500 years ago.

How do we know? What happens if you nudge a spinning top? It wobbles. Early in its history, the earth collided with a planetoid. This collision knocked our planet's axis 23.4 degrees off its upright position. Since then our world has been wobbling along its orbital path around the sun. Right now, the axis points at the North Star. But because of the "nudge," where the axis points changes over time. In the year 3000 BC, the star Thuban was the Pole Star shining right above the North Pole. In about 13,000 years from now, the bright star Vega will become the Pole Star. And 26,000 years from now, the axis will point at what we call Polaris once again.

Polaris, also known as the North Star, is surrounded by large complex dust structures known as molecular clouds or galactic cirrus.

The Birth of the North Star, Okiinaa

One summer night, two young women slept under the stars. They woke just before dawn. Morningstar was glowing in the eastern sky.

"Morningstar is so handsome! I wish he were my husband," said one of them.

The other one laughed. "Dreams like that don't come true."

But Morningstar had heard the young woman's words. He came down to Earth and took her back to the Sky Country to be his wife.

Sun, Morningstar's father, and Moon, Morningstar's mother, accepted the young female human. Moon showed her the chores she should do. Every day they went out with their digging sticks to gather roots for their meals.

One day, the female human noticed a particularly large turnip. "Let's dig it up and take it home to cook," she said.

Moon replied, "It is a holy turnip that grows at the center of our Sky Country. It must stay where it grows."

This made Morningstar's wife curious. She wanted to know why the turnip was so special.

After a time, Morningstar and his human wife had a son. Sun and Moon were delighted with the baby. They named their grandson Okiinaa.

Moon and her daughter-in-law returned to digging roots. One day when the human found herself alone, she happened on the large turnip. Now she was even more curious than before. She used her digging stick to loosen around the edge until she could pull it up. As she did, she saw the hole where the turnip had been. When she looked through the hole, she saw the world below and the camp where her family and friends lived. The sight made her long for her old life.

When she went back to her tipi Morningstar saw the turnip. He knew she had done something very wrong.

"You can no longer live in our Sky Country," he said. "You must return to your people. You will not see Moon when you get back to your camp and your family. You may take Okiinaa with you, but he must not touch the ground until Moon has grown full. Otherwise, Sun will bring him back to the sky and place him in the hole where you pulled out the turnip."

Time-lapsed star trails around Polaris (the Pole Star)

When the female human returned to Earth, she remembered Morningstar's warning. She was careful to always place baby Okiinaa on a buffalo hide so that when he crawled, he would not touch the ground. One day before Moon grew full, the woman left Okiinaa with her mother while she went to gather wood. The boy's grandmother was distracted for a moment. She did not see Okiinaa crawl off the buffalo hide and sit on the ground.

Quickly, she picked him up and cradled him until he fell asleep. She put him back on the hide and covered him over. When her daughter returned, she asked about the baby.

"He is sleeping under that robe," said her mother. But when the woman lifted the blanket there was only a puffball mushroom. She knew at once that Okiinaa had been taken back to the Sky Country.

That night, when the sky grew dark and the Star People appeared, she saw a new star at the center of the sky, a star that did not move. She knew it was Okiinaa, sitting in the hole from which she had pulled the holy turnip. All she could do was hope that Morningstar would look after their son.

MARKING TIME

The regular movements of the sun and the moon were a calendar by which we marked days, months, and years. Unusual occurrences like eclipses, comets, or meteors became historical signposts.

The story of Thunderbird and Raven describes how our seasons came to be.

Thunderbird and Raven

Thunderbird and Raven were two powerful spirits in the Sky Country. They were always eyeing each other suspiciously from their nests atop two of the highest mountain peaks. Thunderbird soared above the land, spreading warm weather. He wanted all the land for himself.

Raven was jealous. "Why should Thunderbird have all the land? I deserve to have time in the sky, too." Raven took flight and brought down snowstorms and icy weather.

This angered Thunderbird. He shot lightning from his eyes at Raven. One lightning bolt struck Raven and singed his feathers black.

So began the battle of the birds. Thunderbird caused thunderstorms as he flapped his wings. Raven would cool the rain and turn it into snow squalls. Thunderbird was about to shoot another lightning bolt at Raven, but Raven flew in a circle and blinded Thunderbird with ice pellets and hailstones.

Days passed and neither could get an advantage over the other. At last they were too exhausted to continue their rivalry, so they decided to share the land. Six moons would be Thunderbird's season. However, Raven used deception to sneak in a few extra days to get seven months for a cold season. The people made a calendar for summer and winter, with the deceptive moon counted as the last one of Raven's season.

Raven Mask, by Marcus Alfred
(Kwakwaka'wakw, 'Namgis First Nation)

My Blackfoot ancestors knew that the moon took about twenty-nine days to wax and wane. It grew from a crescent to a full moon and then diminished to a crescent before it disappeared for four days. With this knowledge they counted the six moons of Thunderbird's summer season and Raven's seven winter moons. The shortest moon cycle of winter has a special name. It is called an "intercalary" or "leap" moon because it is only about ten days long. Every three years those days add up to make a regular moon. Every nation had its own lunar calendar.

The Blackfoot Lunar Calendar

Thunderbird's Season
Ducks return moon
Frog moon
Flowers blossom moon
Long rain moon
Saskatoon berries ripen moon
Prepare food for storage moon

Raven's Season
Deer hunting moon
Ducks leave moon
Cold weather arrives moon
Long night moon
Winter grows old moon
Eagle moon
Deceptive moon

Arc of the Summer Moon in Alberta

Moon Cycle Birds (2019), acrylic on canvas, by Leah Marie Dorian, an interdisciplinary Métis artist raised in Prince Albert, Saskatchewan.

A Blackfoot year was called "one winter." New Winter's Day, the fall equinox, was called *Aahkiaapiksistsiko*, or "going home day." That was the day when they began counting the moons of the new winter. They knew that was when to make plans to travel to the places that would be their homes for the winter.

Government by the Stars

The night sky has enormous spiritual significance. The Skidi, a band of Pawnee people who lived in what is now Nebraska, believed that the stars had human characteristics. They believed that their ancient ancestors were the Star People. The Skidi arranged their homes and lodges to reflect the star group above. Each lodge had an opening on top, not only to let out the smoke from the hearth fire, but so that the "Council" of stars above could be seen clearly, even indoors. A ring of stars in the night sky was called "The Council of Chiefs." Its circle was a symbol of how they were governed. Important decisions were made by the Elders who formed the council circle.

The Pawnee earth lodges were circular, dome-shaped dwellings with heavy timbered framework covered by layers of branches, grass, and lastly earth. A hole was left at the top of the structure to allow smoke from the fireplace to escape, to let in light, and to give the residents a view of the stars. A tunnel-like entry passage extended from one side of the lodge, typically to the east.

This Pawnee Sky Chart was made on tanned elk skin. It represents the star patterns essential to the tribe. Warm orange dye at either end shows where the sun rises and sets. The little star in the middle represents the Milky Way.

Sky Ways of Building

One of the most spectacular examples of how people were guided by sky knowledge can be seen in the colossal structures in Chaco Canyon in northwestern New Mexico. There was little game to hunt nearby, and when Chaco was growing between the 9th and 11th centuries CE, most of the trees were gone. Builders had to travel 80 kilometers (50 miles) to cut down trees. It was backbreaking labor. They had to peel the bark off and let the logs dry before hauling them over treacherous, steep paths home to Chaco Canyon. Why did the Chacoan build there? Why would they live there?

One possible answer is that the buildings were observatories where people could track the movements of the sun and moon so they would know exactly when to plant and harvest, and when to hold religious ceremonies.

The Great House Pueblo Bonito, located in Chaco Culture National Historic Park in Chaco Canyon, New Mexico

The Chacoan built Great Houses four or five stories high with hundreds of rooms, storage buildings, and large ceremonial kivas. A Great House had a number of sight lines to points where the sun and moon would cast similar shadows, perhaps to mirror the way that the gods of Earth and sky come together. Other buildings were aligned with the sun and moon at the solstice and equinox days. Many were also built in line with the four cardinal directions: north, south, east, and west.

The great kiva Casa Rinconada is a nearly perfect circle that may have been a model of the universe, with the walls representing the sky and the ceiling representing the stars. The ledges on the walls were placed in relation to the sun's movement at the equinoxes.

SOLSTICES AND EQUINOXES

The equator is an imaginary line circling the earth that is the same distance from the North and South Poles. It divides the earth into the Northern and Southern Hemispheres.

An equinox occurs when the position of the sun is right over the equator. When this happens, night and day are the same length. The equinox occurs twice each year, once when the sun crosses the equator as it travels north and again when it travels south.

A solstice is a day when the sun is farthest from the equator. The summer solstice is the longest day of the year in the Northern Hemisphere and it occurs in June. The winter solstice is in December and is the shortest day of the year.

A First Nations teenager performs a traditional dance at the Summer Solstice Indigenous Festival for National Indigenous Peoples Day in Vincent Massey Park in Ottawa.

HOPI SUN TRACKERS

A Hopi priest was expected to predict the times of the solstices so people would know when to offer sacrifices for the health of their crops. The priest would go to a sun-watching station to observe the sun as it slowed its path before the solstice. One of these sun-watching stations consisted of a flat stone with a sun face carved on top.

The Solstice Snake is an ancient archeoastronomy site near Moab, Utah. A shadow falls exactly on the snake's head on the summer solstice.

The moon blocks the sun during the total solar eclipse of 2017 near Madras, Oregon.

All over North America eclipses were major events. The Cherokee believed that an eclipse happened when a giant frog was trying to swallow the moon or the sun. For the Hopi, an eclipse was a time of ceremony when people were given sacred names. The Nakoda in Alberta believed that eclipses were omens of things to come. The Elders in Chaco Canyon taught that eclipses were times of transformation and were not to be feared, except by people who had broken a tribal law.

Your day begins like any other. Dawn brushes away the moonless night long before sunrise. Morning keeps its chill until the sun appears. Then you feel its heat. You help your mother grind corn and you make a small fire on the balcony to cook the morning meal. After your family has eaten you help tidy up.

You look up to the bright blue sky rising above the cliff behind the pueblo as you lift a clay jug. Carefully, you climb down to the plaza, pushing aside garlands of dried peppers that hang beside the ladder. You are in no hurry. You pass the great kiva and see smoke curling up beside the ladder propped against the entrance. You are glad to reach the shade of the trees alongside the dry streambed leading to the spring. You dip the jug into the water and let it fill up before you lift it out. You cup your hands in the cool water. You let the water pour down your face and you run your wet fingers through your hair.

When you get up to leave you notice something odd about the light filtering through the leaves. The shadows on the rocks and ground all have crescent shapes. You've never seen such a thing. You start for home. The sky is a darker shade of blue and the sun is not as bright. Your pace quickens. You hear the murmur of voices before you reach the village. Everyone is

MEET THE SKY WATCHERS

Our stories tell us about the Star People who were partly of our world and partly of the Sky Country. A new generation of Blackfoot sky watchers is carrying on that tradition. Like our ancestors they are curious about the meaning of the stars. But unlike our ancestors, who had only eyesight to help them, modern astronomers use telescopes and satellites to discover new knowledge about the universe and our place in it. Now Indigenous scientists are contributing to the world's sky knowledge.

gathered in the plaza, talking anxiously. You find your parents. They are shading their eyes and pointing skyward. You put down the jug and look up, too. You watch the disappearing sun even though the intense light hurts your eyes. Suddenly, the world turns dark. The crowd gasps. You look up at the sky again but instead of the sun you see a black disk with wispy filaments flaring out in all directions. Stars shine where daylight should be.

You are terrified. Maybe an evil spirit has eaten the sun, leaving only darkness forever! Even the priests and your parents are shouting in panic. You think the world is ending.

Then, a miracle. The sun begins to shine again. The stars disappear with the darkness. The sun is as bright and hot as ever. You are confused and relieved. Your father picks up the water jug. You take your mother's hand as you slowly walk back home. There is calm now. You all sit silently on the balcony of your home. You cuddle up to your mother, wondering about the extraordinary day. When night falls your heart pounds the way it does when you wake from a bad dream. You pray with your parents that another ordinary day will dawn.

⊙ ⊙ ⊙

MEET PHYSICIST COREY GRAY AND TRANSLATOR SHARON YELLOWFLY, SIKSIKA NATION, BLACKFOOT

Corey Gray wanted to be MacGyver when he was growing up in southern California, visiting the Siksika Nation during the summers. Instead, he became a physicist. He is the detector operator at the observatory in Hanford, Washington, where the first direct observation of gravitational waves was made in 2015. He was part of the team that discovered the existence of gravitational waves produced when two black holes collide. The discovery opened a whole new way for astronomers to learn about the Sky Country.

Corey Gray wanted to make a connection between his work and his Blackfoot culture—to involve Indigenous youth in astronomy. He started by making information about his work available in the Blackfoot language. Now it is, thanks to his mother, Sharon Yellowfly.

Sharon Yellowfly is translating this cutting-edge information into Blackfoot. She translated terms such as "black hole" by combining the words for "black" and "hole," or *sigooxgiya*. Where new words were needed, she invented them. "Gravitational waves" became "they stick together waves," or *Abuduuxbiisii o?bigimskAAsts*.

The Laser Interferometer Gravitational-Wave Observatory (LIGO) outside of Richland, Washington, on the Hanford Reservation. LIGO detects ripples in space-time by measuring the time it takes laser light to travel between two suspended mirrors.

PLANETARY SCIENTIST AND ASTEROID HUNTER ROB CARDINAL, SIKSIKA NATION

As co-founding Director of the IndigeSTEAM Society, Executive Director of the First Light Initiative, and STEM coordinator at the Siksika Nation Board of Education, Rob Cardinal is eager to preserve cultural traditions and to combine them with technology. First Light introduces Indigenous youth to telescopes, astronomy, and the science of technology of the skies while they are learning and preserving Indigenous sky knowledge.

Rob Cardinal is also an asteroid hunter. One day humans may build a starship to travel into deep space. (A spaceship is a vehicle that flies through outer space; a starship can travel between star systems.) Making starships isn't practical on Earth yet. The solution may be to mine asteroids for raw materials and to build starships in orbit.

Rob Cardinal is one of the astronomers who is searching for near-Earth objects like asteroids that could be mined. He also has a comet named after him.

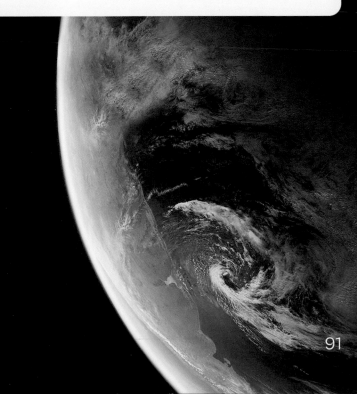

From our earliest astronomers to our modern astrophysicists, we have recognized the sacred gifts of the sky. The skies are our maps, our calendars, and our guides for building our communities.

Indigenous knowledge is braided together from our stories, the teachings of Elders and Knowledge Keepers, and our own observations, inventions, and shared ideas. There have been many times in our history when we might have lost our body of knowledge. In the next chapter meet some of the people who are making sure that it is never forgotten.

Keeping the Knowledge

Inuit singer and storyteller Tiffany Ayalik of the musical group Quantum Tangle tells a scary Inuit tale at the Canmore Folk Music Festival in Canmore, Alberta.

Indigenous people hold their oral narratives in high esteem because that was the way we passed knowledge from one generation to the next. Although there were graphic traditions that used symbols to express ideas, only in Mexico did a true writing system develop. People made their own observations and gained experience from their encounters with the world. However, passing on their wisdom was not a matter of reciting and memorizing facts. Stories and storytelling were dependable methods for transmitting the information that became our folklore, mainly because they braided learning with entertainment. Even today, people will remember an event or fact if it provokes a strong emotional reaction such as a good laugh or a good cry.

HOW WE REMEMBER

While a good memory is essential for oral history and stories, narrators often used mnemonic devices to help them remember the details of a saga. When passing knowledge on to new generations, Elders communicated with picture writing, symbols, and images in much the same way that we transmit information with icons and emojis today.

The Power of Stories

Narratives have tremendous power because everybody loves a good story. Storytellers must have great memories to recall the details of action and characters, but they must also be entertaining to keep their audiences entranced. When they recall tales of adventure, they can transport you to the fantastic places of your imagination, or they can make you share the joys, worries, and fears of fictional characters. Stories can even help you navigate danger in uncertain situations.

Nuu-Chah-Nulth people made ocean-going canoes that carried them far out of sight of land. They needed effective geographical information to find their way back to their coastal villages, but they did not draw maps. Their solution? They created stories that contained details of their mental maps of the coastline's bays, inlets, and prominent headlands. If heavy fog and weather were to obscure their view they could recall a "transformer" story that described landmarks in the correct order as they paddled along the coast in canoes. Story maps preserved the details of the coastline so they could find their safe route home.

TRANSFORMER BEINGS

Transformer beings in our stories turn humans into features on the landscape. Visitors to Vancouver, British Columbia, cannot miss the two peaks dominating the North Shore Mountains. Although we know them as "the Lions," Squamish storytellers call them the Twin Sisters. They were known as peacemakers who worked tirelessly to bring warring tribes together. For their efforts the Sky Beings transformed them into mountain peaks so they could always watch over their homeland.

This wampum belt, from around the 17th century, is made of shell beads and hemp and comes from the American Iroquoian or Algonquian nations.

Memory Aids: *Itimat* and Wampum

On the Columbia plateau that stretches across Washington, Oregon, and Idaho, people used an *itimat*, a hemp string "time ball" that was like a diary. The string was tied with tiny markers of colored stones, bones, beads, and cloth that were records of major events in an individual's life.

In the Northeast, wampum belts made from seashell beads were used to mark important matters like treaties. The designs and colors were a record that later councils used to remember decisions.

THE HISTORICAL RECORD

People in North America recorded important events with symbols, pictographs (paintings), and petroglyphs (carvings). In Mexico people wrote their history for thousands of years on paper, pottery, and stone monuments. Four different historical records come from the Piikani, Aztecs, Anishinaabe, and Cherokee.

Petroglyph panels such as the one below used picture writing to transmit the details of oral history. This petroglyph panel is from southeastern Utah, near the old Anasazi community called Hovenweep. It dates back to Anasazi time.

These petroglyphs of bighorn sheep come from the Anasazi culture and are found in Arizona's Monument Valley Tribal Park.

The Winter Count

Many people on the Plains kept a winter count recorded in pictographs (pictures or symbols used for words) painted on an animal hide. Every community could have several versions of a winter count. Individuals also used a winter count to record big events in their own lives.

The oldest surviving winter count is on a buffalo hide from 1761. It tells us that five years into this winter count, berries stayed on the trees all winter. It records the year when there was hail and thunder in the winter, and the years when the buffalo and antelope got sick after an eclipse, among many more events.

The winter count is a record of our history: memorable events such as the arrival of guns, metal pots, wagons, and the Royal Canadian Mounted Police (RCMP), and the signing of treaties might become the name of a winter.

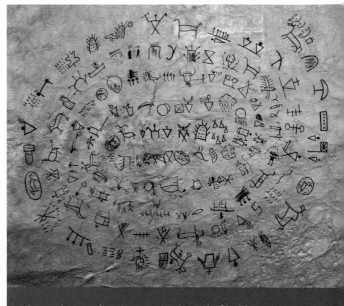

A reproduction of a winter count robe in the Blackfoot Native Tribes exhibit, at the Head-Smashed-In Buffalo Jump Interpretive Centre, near Fort Macleod, Alberta

Aztec Libraries

The people of Mexico and Central America wrote thousands of books that were painted on paper pounded from tree bark and then folded like an accordion. They were colorful: reds came from cochineal (squashed cactus beetle), blues from herb-blossom, chili red and dark green from trees, black from pine pitchwood smoke. Priest-scribes created even more colors by adding rock ochres, chalk, sour fruit, vegetable oil, and brown tree moss. They used brushes to write science books, biographies of great people, detailed family histories, instruction manuals for how to perform rituals, and collections of songs and poetry. They recorded the taxes collected for fine cloth, military uniforms, feathered headdresses, plants, and bundles of blankets.

When the Spanish arrived, they burned down whole libraries. Only a few of the books survived, now carefully archived in museums. Despite this loss we know a lot about their history because potters drew historical narratives on their pottery. Artists carved the chronicles of kings and heroes onto the stone of their buildings and public monuments. Fortunately for us, the Spanish priests could not destroy the history carved in stone.

The *Wiigwaasabakoon*

Anishinaabeg who lived around Lake Superior used a stylus of bone or wood to inscribe geometric forms on birchbark scrolls. These *Wiigwaasabakoon* contain accounts of supernatural forces that occupied the land and waters of the Great Lakes. The Midewiwin is an Anishinaabeg society that also uses birchbark scrolls that recall songs, sacred healing practices, and medicines. The sacred scrolls are still used by those who are entrusted to read them properly.

Stories recalled in the Midewiwin scrolls became the inspiration for the renowned Anishinaabeg artist Norval Morrisseau. His traditional name was Copper Thunderbird and his youth was an immersion in Anishinaabeg language and culture that would find expression through art. He imitated the techniques found on the Midewiwin scrolls to produce some of his earliest works. He scraped off layers of birchbark to reveal the different hues that created images of spirit beings. His work inspired a generation of Indigenous artists who became known collectively as the Woodlands School of Art. He used birchbark throughout his young career because he was too poor to afford the oils, acrylics, brushes, and canvas that artists need. When the art world discovered Morrisseau, he started to earn enough money to purchase the proper equipment suitable for an artist. After his death, those birchbark panels he scraped at to render his fantastic imaginings became coveted artworks that sell for over half a million dollars.

Storyteller of the Ages (1970), acrylic on canvas, by Norval Morrisseau. Known as the "Picasso of the North," Norval Morrisseau created works depicting the legends of his people, the cultural and political tensions between Indigenous and European traditions, and his deep spirituality and mysticism.

The *Cherokee Phoenix*

Sequoyah made a unique contribution to the way Cherokee people understood their language, because he introduced them to literacy. Until he showed his alphabet to his relatives in 1821, they only knew Cherokee by the spoken word. Once Sequoyah taught his family and a few friends to write their speech, the practice took hold in the community.

Only seven years later there were enough Cherokee who were literate in their mother tongue and in English that they could launch a community newspaper in both languages. The *Cherokee Phoenix* was the first newspaper published by Indigenous people in the United States, and the first published in an Indigenous language. The first issue came out in English and Cherokee on February 21, 1828, in New Echota, the capital of the Cherokee Nation in present-day Georgia. It featured news of the day, laws, and public documents using the Cherokee alphabet invented by Sequoyah.

A painting by Charles Bird King from around 1825 of John Ridge, Cherokee leader and publisher of the *Cherokee Phoenix*

The name changed to the *Cherokee Phoenix and Indians' Advocate* in 1829. Issues of the newspaper are a priceless record of a dark time. Cherokee citizens read the paper anxiously for news as the U.S. Supreme Court heard cases about their rights to their own land. In 1830 the newspaper reported the news that the Supreme Court had issued a judgment in their favor. However, in spite of that decision, President Andrew Jackson had signed the Indian Removal Act into law. As a result the Cherokee were forced to leave their ancestral homeland and walk to another home in Indian Territory west of the Mississippi (present-day Oklahoma) on the Trail of Tears. White settlers broke into the newspaper office and destroyed the printing presses.

The *Cherokee Phoenix* was revived in the 20th century. Today readers can read either a print or electronic version.

UNDERSTANDING KNOWLEDGE THAT'S HELD IN LANGUAGE

Indigenous knowledge is transmitted by word of mouth, so it can't be unbraided from our languages. In the United States, three hundred Indigenous languages are spoken, but over one hundred are already extinct. Of the seventy Indigenous languages spoken in Canada, only three (Cree, Ojibwe, and Inuktitut) are projected to persist deep into the 21st century. As each language goes silent, so too does all the wisdom it once transmitted between generations.

Our experience teaches us that to avoid a mass extinction of Indigenous languages, we must be creative and use any technology to keep our speech vibrant. Indigenous people are teaching and taking language classes using the age-old methods of oral tradition. Elders are leading conversation classes, teaching at Indigenous-language schools, and writing literature. As a native speaker of Blackfoot, I too worry that there is no future for my language. However, as a professor in a modern university I have access to resources that are not available to most people. Therefore I began a research partnership with my computer science colleagues to employ the power of artificial intelligence and robotics to ensure that Blackfoot remains a dynamic, modern language. Our first products will be chatbots that introduce students to the sounds, words, and phrases that will help them learn enough Blackfoot to carry on a conversation.

PLAINS SIGN LANGUAGE

When people on the Plains traveled from what is now Saskatchewan to as far away as Texas to hunt, trade, or go on pilgrimages, they passed through many nations where people spoke different languages. Plains Sign Language was a way for people who spoke different languages to communicate with one another.

Today people are keen to preserve this method of communication. At Plains Sign Language camp at Poundmaker Cree Nation near Cut Knife, Saskatchewan, students have come from Alberta, Nova Scotia, New Zealand, and Poland to learn it.

Lanny Real Bird is from the Crow Nation in Montana and he teaches Plains Sign Language this past summer at a multi-day language camp at Poundmaker Cree Nation.

MEET

LANGUAGE KEEPER MARIE WILCOX, WUKCHUMNI

Marie Wilcox was born in 1933. As time passed and friends and family died, she realized that she was the only person left who could speak Wukchumni fluently (Wukchumni was spoken along the Tule and Kaweah Rivers of Central California.) There is no record of written Wukchumni, so she set out to write a dictionary. From early morning to late at night, she typed out one Wukchumni word after another on her computer. She took seven years, and her dictionary was published in 2014 so others could also learn the language.

Marie Wilcox and her daughter Jennifer now teach Wukchumni language classes. Wukchumni is spoken once again among family and community members, happy that they can hold conversations, ask questions, and tell jokes in their mother tongue.

A Message from "Long Ago Person Found":
The Knowledge That's Held in Crafts

In 1999, a group of hunters found the body of a young man in a crevasse in Tatshenshini-Alsek Provincial Park in northern British Columbia. His body had melted out of a glacier about six hundred years after he died. His skull was found in 2003.

In the Tutchone language of the Champagne and Aishihik First Nations (whose lands cover part of the Yukon and northern British Columbia, where he died), Kwäday Dän Ts'ìnchi̧ means "Long Ago Person Found." He had stone tools and a spear thrower with him, so he was probably a hunter. He carried a pouch full of dried salmon. His last meal of shellfish and beach asparagus indicates that he was on the coast only a few hours before his death on the glacier.

When he was found, Long Ago Person Found was wearing a cape made from the pelts of a hundred ground squirrels. He also wore a wide-brimmed hat woven from spruce roots.

That hat meant a lot to weaver Delores Churchill.

WEAVER DELORES CHURCHILL, HAIDA

Indigenous knowledge principles inform the weavings created by Ilskyalas Delores Churchill. For instance, she uses the natural materials, such as spruce root, that her grandmothers once used. The spruce root comes from a living tree, so she makes her weaving as beautiful as she can to honor the tree's gift. She takes the root from the tree carefully so that other plants aren't disturbed. She makes sure not to harm the tree so that future generations can use it for weaving.

Delores Churchill wanted to learn about Long Ago Person Found's hat as a way to respect the weaver who had made it and the generations of weavers who have passed along the craft to her.

Clans usually don't share their basket-making techniques. However, Delores worried that the art of basketry was dying out. She went to Elders in different communities to ask if she could learn their way of weaving and share it with other artisans. The Elders agreed.

The Champagne and Aishihik, the descendants of Long Ago Person Found, restrict access to the hat out of respect for the long-dead young man. However, they allowed Delores to see it. She knew what to look for. If the weaving were counterclockwise, she could tell it was Haida. Clockwise, the weaver was Tlingit. When she looked at the hat closely, she realized that the weaver had known both Haida and Tlingit ways. The nations must have exchanged ideas.

Parts of the hat were frayed. Did that mean that it was older than the young man? Had his grandmother made it for him? Had his father worn it? Or did rain or sun erode the artist's handiwork?

Delores Churchill took part in a DNA study that showed that she and the young man in the ground squirrel cloak shared a direct ancestor. That was fascinating, but she already knew the connection: it was the history woven into the hat.

The Knowledge Keeper

MEET

KNOWLEDGE KEEPER KWAXSISTALLA, KAWADILLIKALL CLAN OF THE DZAWATAINUK TRIBE OF THE KWAKWAKA'WAK FIRST NATION, 1929–2019

Kwaxsistalla's people were from the Northwest Coast. Their children were being sent to residential schools where they were forbidden from speaking their own language, wearing traditional clothes, or practicing traditional ways.

The Elders were afraid that their way of life would be lost. They decided that somebody had to hold the people's knowledge. They chose Kwaxsistalla (Adam Dick). Two Chiefs took Kwaxsistalla upriver in a canoe and kept him hidden from government officials.

The Elders taught him at least five hundred songs that described his people's history and spiritual connections. They also taught him food-gathering knowledge. He learned about root gardens and how to dig for clover roots, cinquefoil roots, rice roots, and lupine roots. He knew about burying the main root so it would grow again. He was taught how to roll rocks to the beach and make a clam garden. Potlatch is an important ceremony and gift-giving feast in the Northwest. It was banned in 1885 by the Canadian government. When the ban was lifted in 1951, it was Kwaxsistalla who could teach everyone the proper practices.

Kwaxsistalla was recognized all over the world as the respected Knowledge Keeper of his people, and as the teacher of new generations who will keep the knowledge alive.

Sky Wolf's Call

Thousands of years ago, a few friendly wolves first visited our camps and joined us in the hunt. They began to trust us. Eventually some of them started living with us and became our friends. No wonder people liked to tell stories about them. My Piikani ancestors told stories about Makoyi, the Chief of the Wolves. Makoyi was a story-figure who was a friend and protector. He and the Sky Wolves taught us how to hunt and how to sing (to this day when the drumming starts, the people dance to the wolf's howls) and because wolves are not solitary animals, they continue to remind us about the importance of living in harmony with one another.

The Sky Wolf's story connects the skies with the earth, people with animals, the practical with the spiritual. Understanding the idea of connections is an important lesson these days. The challenges of climate change, pandemics, and wars affect everybody, and solutions only come when we all work together.

Indigenous knowledge is based on the idea that this world is a gift. The Sky Wolves took pity on us and gave us special gifts to keep. What a reminder to cherish the gifts we've been given! We are taught to take care of our waters, to use fire wisely, to grow food so that it will feed us and those who will come after us, to build wisely, and to keep ourselves, our communities, and our world in harmony.

Finally, we are reminded to give thanks. We give thanks for the Sky Wolves' gifts—and for the gifts of the Three Sisters, the Buffalo, the Beaver, and the other animals that share our world. When we sing and dance and celebrate, we are reminded of our duty to give back. Indigenous knowledge is not only for Indigenous people. The wisdom it holds can help the whole world. Can you imagine what the world would be like for every living being if everybody had this knowledge? Think of how we would treat the earth and the plants, the animals and water, and each other. This is knowledge that has served Indigenous people well since time began. It can help us all find our way in the future.

A Piikani Fancy Shawl dancer performs a traditional dance on the Prairies at Head-Smashed-in-Buffalo-Jump World Heritage Site in Fort Macleod, Alberta.

Thanks and Acknowledgments

To Api'soomaahka (William Singer III), our grateful thanks for your careful reading of the text and your comments.

And to Rivka Cranley, Chandra Wohleber, Lisa Frenette, Tania Craan, and Mary Rose MacLachlan, your support and work have been invaluable.

As always, to Bill Harnum, your support and encouragement mean everything.

Thank you to those who have given their time and offered their knowledge so generously:

Dr. Kyle Bobiwash (entomologist), Anishinaabe Nation

Amy Cardinal Christianson (fire research scientist), Métis Nation of Alberta

Rob Cardinal (planetary scientist), Siksika Nation, Blackfoot

Dr. Lindsay Crowshoe (medicine man), Piikani

Craig Falcon (sweat lodge Knowledge Keeper), Blackfoot

Corey Gray (astrophysicist), Siksika Nation, Blackfoot

Roger Lewis (curator of Mi'kmaq Cultural Heritage at the Nova Scotia Museum), Mi'kmaw, Sipekne'katik, Shubenacadie

Clayton Shirt, Saddle Lake Cree (traditional healer), Treaty 6, Potawatomi

Dr. Esther Tailfeathers (medicine woman), Kainai

Sharon Yellowfly (translator), Siksika Nation, Blackfoot

Glossary

Aquaculture Aquaculture involves cultivating fish, mollusks, and aquatic plants under controlled conditions.

Astronomy Astronomy is the study of celestial objects and things that appear in the sky, like stars, planets, the sun, the moon, nebulae, galaxies, and comets.

Band A band is a small, self-governing group that bases its membership on family connections. In Canada a band has a legal meaning as a political unit occupying an "Indian reserve," though we now call them First Nations.

Buffalo/Bison The scientific name for the American bison is *Bison bison*, and the European bison, or wisent, is known as the *Bison bonasus*. These are the only species of bison. There are tropical buffalo in Africa and Asia, so many people use the word "bison" to avoid confusion with them. Both "buffalo" and "bison" are correct and refer to the big, shaggy animals that live in North America.

Climate Change Climate change refers to a change in global or regional climate patterns. Today the increased levels of carbon dioxide produced by the use of fossil fuels such as coal, petroleum, and natural gas result in a warming climate.

Cultural Burns Controlled burns are carefully planned fires that are set when there is little risk to people. Prescribed burns get rid of pine needles, dead leaves, grasses, twigs, and fallen trees that could fuel wildfires. Cultural burns are used to benefit the land.

Dam A dam is a barrier that is built to stop or hold back water. This raises the water level, forming a reservoir. The water in the reservoir can be used for many things: to generate electricity, as a water supply for drinking, or for industrial use like aquaculture.

Etuapmumk *Etuapmumk* means "two-eyed seeing" in the Mi'kmaq language. One eye sees with the strengths of Indigenous ways of knowing, and the other sees a scientific worldview. *Etuapmumk* means learning to use both eyes together for the benefit of all.

Gadugi *Gadugi* is a Cherokee principle that means "working together for the community."

Inuit/Inuk Inuit are a group of people who live in the Arctic parts of Greenland, Canada, and Alaska. "Inuit" means "The People" and refers to the group. The word "Inuk" refers to an individual.

Kiva A kiva is an underground ceremonial room used for religious ceremonies by the Indigenous people of the Southwest.

Métis Métis people have historical lineage rooted in the areas of land in west central North America. The traditional languages spoken by Métis people include Michif and Cree.

Nation "Nation" refers to a group of people who are identified with a particular territory.

Netukulimk The Mi'kmaq term *Netukulimk* means "take only what is needed and waste nothing."

The Trail of Tears In 1838 the Cherokee were rounded up and forced off their land in Georgia. In the dead of winter, they were forced to walk all the way to Oklahoma, about 3,200 kilometers (2,000 miles) away. At least three thousand died. This tragedy is called the Trail of Tears.

Tribe "Tribe" describes a collection of bands connected by kinship, politics, and language. The United States uses "tribe" as a legal term for a political unit associated with an "Indian reservation."

Weir A weir is a low rock wall or wooden fence built across a river or stream to trap fish as they migrate upstream. A weir is built to intercept fish where water flows out of lakes or where rivers empty into the ocean.

Selected Reading

Websites

Canadian Museum of History, https://www.historymuseum.ca.

Columbia River Inter-Tribal Fish Commission, https://www.critfc.org.

Defenders of Wildlife, https://defenders.org.

Good Fire (podcast) Amy Cardinal Christianson and Matthew Kristoff, https://yourforestpodcast.com/good-fire-podcast.

Laser Interferometer Gravitational-Wave Observatory (LIGO), https://www.ligo.caltech.ed.

National Museum of the American Indian, Smithsonian Institution, https://americanindian.si.edu.

Books

Aikenhead, Glen, and Herman Michell. *Bridging Cultures: Indigenous and Scientific Ways of Knowing Nature*. Toronto: Pearson Canada, 2011.

Davis, Wade. *The Wayfinders: Why Ancient Wisdom Matters in the Modern World*. Toronto: House of Anansi Press, 2009.

Jemison, G. Peter, and Anna M. Schein, eds. *The Treaty of Canandaigua 1794: 200 Years of Treaty Relations between the Iroquois Confederacy and the United States*. Santa Fe: Clear Light, 2000.

Kimmerer, Robin Wall. *Braiding Sweetgrass: Indigenous Wisdom, Scientific Knowledge, and the Teachings of Plants*. Minneapolis: Milkweed Editions, 2013.

Kimmerer, Robin Wall. *Gathering Moss: A Natural and Cultural History of Mosses*. Corvallis, OR: Oregon State University Press, 2003.

Lacey, Laurie. *Mi'kmaq Medicines: Remedies and Recollections*. Halifax: Nimbus Publishing, 1993, 2012.

McMillan, Alan D., and Eldon Yellowhorn. *First Peoples in Canada*. Vancouver: Douglas & McIntyre, 2004.

Nelson, Melissa K., ed. *Original Instructions: Indigenous Teachings for a Sustainable Future*. Rochester, VT: Bear & Company, 2008.

Watson, Julia. *Lo—TEK: Design by Radical Indigenism*. Cologne, Germany: TASCHEN, 2019.

Wissler, Clark, and D. C. Duvall. "Mythology of the Blackfoot Indians." In *Anthropological Papers of the American Museum of Natural History*, vol. 2, part 1. New York: Order of the Trustees, 1908.

Yellowhorn, Eldon. "Calling Down the Spirits in the Sky: Blackfoot Astronomy and Sense of the Sacred." In *Intersections of Religion and Astronomy,* edited by Aaron Ricker, Christopher J. Corbally and Darry Dinnell. New York: Routledge, 2021.

Yellowhorn, Eldon, and Kathy Lowinger. *Turtle Island: The Story of North America's First People*. Toronto: Annick Press, 2017.

Yellowhorn, Eldon, and Kathy Lowinger. *What the Eagle Sees: Indigenous Stories of Rebellion and Renewal*. Toronto: Annick Press, 2019.

Sources and Contacts

Andersen, Chamois. "The Return of the Buffalo to Fort Peck." *Wild without End* (blog), Defenders of Wildlife, October 2, 2019. https://defenders.org/blog/2019/10/return-of-buffalo-fort-peck.

Buono, Page. "The Fire We Need." *High Country News*, April 24, 2020. https://www.hcn.org/articles/south-wildfire-the-fire-we-need.

Cardinal Christianson, A., N. Caverley, D. Diabo, K. Ellsworth, B. Highway, J. Jonas, S. Joudry, L. L'Hirondelle, W. Skead, M. Vandevord, and R. Ault. *Blazing the Trail: Celebrating Indigenous Fire Stewardship*. Sherwood Park, AB: FireSmart Canada, 2020.

Columbia River Inter-Tribal Fish Commission. "We Are All Salmon People." https://www.critfc.org/salmon-culture/we-are-all-salmon-people/.

Cardinal Christianson, A., N. Caverley, D. Diabo, K. Ellsworth, B. Highway, J. Jonas, S. Joudry, L. L'Hirondelle, W. Skead, M. Vandevord, and R. Ault. *Blazing the Trail: Celebrating Indigenous Fire Stewardship*. Sherwood Park, AB: FireSmart Canada, 2020.

Hance, Jeremy. "How Native American Tribes Are Bringing Back the Bison from Brink of Extinction." *Guardian*, December 12, 2018. https://www.theguardian.com/environment/2018/dec/12/how-native-american-tribes-are-bringing-back-the-bison-from-brink-of-extinction.

Hilleary, Cecily. "Veterans With PTSD Find Relief in Native American Rituals." *VOA News*, March 22, 2018. https://www.voanews.com/a/veterans-with-ptsd-find-relief-in-native-american-rituals/4308945.html.

Jemison, G. Peter, and Anna M. Schein, eds. *The Treaty of Canandaigua 1794: 200 Years of Treaty Relations between the Iroquois Confederacy and the United States*. Santa Fe: Clear Light, 2000.

Joudry, Shalan. "Puktewei: Learning from Fire in Mi'kma'ki (Mi'kmaq Territory)." Master's thesis, Dalhousie University, 2016. https://dalspace.library.dal.ca/bitstream/handle/10222/72599/Joudry-Shalan-MES-SRES-August-2016.pdf?sequence=5.

Morrison, Jim. "An Ancient People with a Modern Climate Plan." *Washington Post*, November 24, 2020. https://www.washingtonpost.com/climate-solutions/2020/11/24/native-americans-climate-change-swinomish/?arc404=true.

The Ontario Human Rights Commission. "Policy on Preventing Discrimination Based on Creed." Approved by the OHRC on September 17, 2015. http://www.ohrc.on.ca/en/policy-preventing-discrimination-based-creed.

Rannie, W. F. "The 'Grass Fire Era' on the Southeastern Canadian Prairies." In *Prairie Perspectives: Geographical Essays*, vol. 4. Prairie Division, Canadian Association of Geographers, 2001. https://pcag.uwinnipeg.ca/Prairie-Perspectives/PP-Vol04/Rannie.pdf.

Vancouver Aboriginal Transformative Justice Services Society. "Who We Are." http://vatjss.com/what-we-do.

Zotigh, Dennis W. "American Indian Beliefs about the Eclipse." *Smithsonian Voices* (blog), National Museum of the American Indian. *Smithsonian*, August 21, 2017. https://www.smithsonianmag.com/blogs/national-museum-american-indian/2017/08/21/american-indian-beliefs-about-eclipse.

Image Credits

Cover: (man) Danita Delimont / Alamy Stock Photo; (wolf) Taylor/Unsplash; (moon cycle) Adam Dutton/Unsplash

Title Page: Design Pics Inc / Alamy Stock Photo

Author's Note: 4 Jonathan Larson / Unsplash

Chapter 1: 5 Chris Cheadle / All Canada Photos; 6 (top) Photo by Diana Chan. Courtesy of Bella Bella Community School; (bottom) *Tree of Life*, by Donald Chrétien (Anishinaabe), acrylic on canvas. Reprinted with permission of the artist; 7 (top) Frye Art Museum, Founding Collection, Gift of Charles and Emma Frye, 1952.135; (bottom) Patrick Tomek / Shutterstock.com; 8 (background) Ihnatovich Maryia / Shutterstock.com; © Citizen Potawatomi Nation; 9 (top) nature photos / Shutterstock.com; (bottom) © Frank Vaisvilas — USA TODAY NETWORK; 10 (top) robertharding / Alamy Stock Photo; (bottom) Panther Media GmbH / Alamy Stock Photo; 11 (top) © Brooklyn Museum of Art / Museum Collection Fund / Bridgeman Images (bottom) Ruth Bonneville / Winnipeg Free Press; (illustration) Nattle / Shutterstock.com; 12 (top) Courtesy of Unama'ki Institute of Natural Resources; (bottom) ArcticPhoto / All Canada Photos; 13 Nativestock.com / Marilyn Angel Wynn / Alamy Stock Photo; 14–15 Siim Lukka / Unsplash; 15 Eye Ubiquitous / Alamy Stock Photo; 16 Alan Dyer / VWPics / Alamy Stock Photo

Chapter 2: 17 Jeffrey Workman / Unsplash; 18 agefotostock / Alamy Stock Photo; 19 RGB Ventures / SuperStock / Alamy Stock Photo; 20 Illustration by Robert B. Ciaccio, Courtesy of Desert Archaeology, Inc; 21 (top) Cayman / Alamy Stock Photo; (bottom) Courtesy of the Nova Scotia Museum; 22 © Neily Trappman Studio; 23 (inset) Todd Klassy Photography; (bottom) Wheateater / Wikimedia; 24 Buddy Mays / Alamy Stock Photo; 25 (left) Puffin's Pictures / Alamy Stock Photo; (right) *Globe and Mail* / CP Images; 26 (top) Courtesy of Seneca Nation; (bottom) woodsnorthphoto / Shutterstock.com; 27 THE CANADIAN PRESS / John Woods; 28 THE CANADIAN PRESS / John Woods; 29 (top) UN Photo / Manuel Elías; (bottom) Courtesy of Stephanie Peltier; (background) CPD-Lab / Shutterstock.com; 30 Robert Ritchie / Unsplash

Chapter 3: 31 Nature's Charm / Shutterstock.com; 32 Anders Ryman / Alamy Stock Photo; 35 (top) Amelia Martin / Shutterstock.com; (center) NataMyr / Shutterstock.com; (bottom left) Oleg Shakirov / Shutterstock.com; (bottom right) Food Impressions / Shutterstock.com; 36 (top) xhico / Shutterstock.com; (bottom) AP Photo / Manuel Valdes; 37 (top) meanderingemu / Alamy Stock Photo; (bottom) Photo courtesy of the Toronto Catholic District School Board; 38 (top) Courtesy of UBC Museum of Anthropology, Dene pipe, Object A2.229. Photograph by Kyla Bailey; (bottom) Sunny Celeste / Alamy Stock Photo; 39 *Navajo Fire Dance*, by Beatien Yazz (1928–2013). Courtesy of the Toddy Family; 40 (top) ArcticPhoto / All Canada Photos; (bottom) Denise Titian / *Ha-Shilth-Sa*; 41 Courtesy of Amy Cardinal Christianson; 42–34 Courtesy of Yukon First Nations Wildfire; 44 © Kiliii Yüyan, Photographer; 45 (top) Fort Apache Agency; (bottom left) Ryan Hagerty, USFWS; (bottom right) Image Courtesy of David Hocs; 46 Landon Parenteau / Unsplash

Chapter 4: 47 Nature Picture Library / Alamy Stock Photo; 49 Heritage Image Partnership Ltd / Alamy Stock Photo; 50 (top) *Untitled (Buffalo Spirit)* by Garnet Tobacco (Cree). Image courtesy of Coastal Peoples Fine Arts Gallery; 50–51 (illustration) Vladimir Zyankin / Dreamstime.com;

51 (top) NPS Photo / Alamy Stock Photo; (bottom) Design Pics Inc / Alamy Stock Photo; 52 © Mikhail Crispin; (illustration) Ivan Kotliar / Dreamstime.com; 53 (top) Farid Rahemtulla; (bottom) Danita Delimont Creative / Alamy Stock Photo; 54 Fort Folly Habitat Recovery (illustration) Ivan Kotliar / Dreamtime.com; 55 Joe Mabel / Wikimedia / CC BY-SA 3.0; 56 Boomer Jerritt / All Canada Photos; 57 Double Brain / Shutterstock.com; 58 *Sky Woman*, oil painting, Ernest Smith (1907–1975), Tonawanda Reservation, 1936. From the Rochester Museum & Science Center, Rochester, NY; 59 (top) © Mikhail Crispin; (bottom) Conrad Barrington / Shutterstock.com; 60 (left) ravipat / Shutterstock.com; (right) Lena Wurm / Shutterstock.com; 61 (top) ZUMA Press Inc / Alamy Stock Photo; (bottom) Maggie Sully / Alamy Stock Photo; 62 Aaron Burden / Unsplash; 63 AP Photo / Amy Forliti; 64 (top) Courtesy of Kyle Bobiwash; (bottom) Milada Vigerova / Unsplash

Chapter 5: 65 Fritz Mueller Visuals; 66 (top) Markus Winkler / Unsplash; (bottom) © Michele Cornelius / Dreamstime.com; 67 Danita Delimont / Shutterstock.com; 68 Hemis / Alamy Stock Photo; 69 (top) Courtesy of Wingspan Media; (bottom) THE CANADIAN PRESS / Graham Hughes; 70 (boy) Danita Delimont / Alamy Stock Photo; (stone) agefotostock / Alamy Stock Photo; 71 (top) Courtesy of Dr. Lindsay Crowshoe, (bottom) Courtesy of Dr. Esther Tailfeathers. Photo provided by Alberta Medical Association; 72 © Morgan Heim; 73 (left) Science History Images / Alamy Stock Photo; (right) Pacific Stock / All Canada Photos; 74 Pat Kane Photo; 75 Kevin Brusie Photography; (background) nature photos / Shutterstock.com; 76 Bart van Meele / Unsplash

Chapter 6: 77 Vincent Guth / Unsplash; 78 *Ancestors* by Brit Ellis/Blue Hummingbird courtesy of the artist. Photographer Brendan Ouelllette, Annick Press; 79 © Bray Falls / NASA; 81 Saman Ziyaie / Unsplash; 82 *Raven Mask* by Marcus Alfred, (Kwakwaka'wakw, 'Namgis Nation). Image courtesy of Coastal Peoples Fine Arts Gallery; 83 Stocktrek Images, Inc. / Alamy Stock Photo; 84 *Moon Cycle Birds*, 2019. Copyright © Leah Dorion. Reprinted with permission of the artist; 85 (left) Heritage Image Partnership Ltd / Alamy Stock Photo; (right) Edward S. Curtis Collection / Library of Congress; 86 kojihirano / Shutterstock.com; 87 (top) Paul McKinnon / Alamy Stock Photo; (bottom) Timothy Mulholland / Alamy Stock Photo; 88 (top) Jeremy Thies / Shutterstock.com; 88–89 maleo113/Shutterstock.com; 89 (top) © Allexxandar / Shutterstock.com; 90 (top) Courtesy of Corey Gray; (bottom) Joseph Becker / Alamy Stock Photo; 91 Courtesy of Rob Cardinal; 92 Fabian Oelkers / Unsplash

Chapter 7: 93 © Jeff Bassett; 94 (top) Danita Delimont / Alamy Stock Photo; (bottom) Paul Vazquez / Unsplash; 95 karamysh / Shutterstock; 96 (top) © Ashmolean Museum / Bridgeman Images; (bottom) Larry Geddis / Alamy Stock Photo; 97 Witold Skrypczak / Alamy Stock Photo; 98 © Fred Jones Jr. Museum of Art / Gift of Dr. and Mrs. R. E. Mansfield, 2003 / Bridgeman Images; 99 (top) Library of Congress Prints and Photographs Division; (bottom) Historic Images / Alamy Stock Photo; 101 (top) Ntawnis Piapot / CBC Licensing; (bottom) Tommy Lee Kreger / CC Attribution 2.0 Generic License; 102 Wikipedia / Tobias Klenze / CC-BY-SA 4.0; 103 Images courtesy of First Peoples Fund. Photography by Hulleah Tsinhnahjinnie (Seminole-Muscogee-Navajo); 104 Photograph by Ecotrust. Permission granted by Kim Recalma-Clutesi

Chapter 8: 105 Don Johnston / All Canada Photos; 106 Don Johnston / All Canada Photos; 107 John E. Marriott / All Canada Photos

Index